Celebrating the
National Reading Initiative

BOOKS

Some books are full of pictures,
Some books are very small,
Some books are thin and some are thick,
If I were asked to answer quick,
I'd say, "I like them all."

Romney Gay

Publishing Information

Celebrating the National Reading Initiative was edited and prepared for photo-offset reproduction by the staff of the Bureau of Publications, California State Department of Education, and was published by the Department, 721 Capitol Mall, Sacramento, California (mailing address: P.O. Box 944272, Sacramento, CA 94244-2720). It was printed by the Office of State Printing and distributed under the provisions of the Library Distribution Act and *Government Code* Section 11096.

Paul Lee, Senior Graphic Artist, created the original artwork that appears in the body of this publication, and Marguerite Wobschall, Senior Graphic Artist, designed the format.

Additional copies of this publication are available for $6.75 each, plus sales tax for California purchasers, from Bureau of Publications, Sales Unit, California State Department of Education, P.O. Box 271, Sacramento, CA 95802-0271. A partial list of other publications available from the Department appears on page 86. A complete list of departmental publications can be obtained by writing to the address given above.

For additional information about the National Reading Initiative, call Francie Alexander, Associate Superintendent, Curriculum, Instruction, and Assessment Division, (916) 322-0498, or Shirley Hazlett, Consultant in Language Arts, (916) 322-3284; or write to Ms. Alexander or Ms. Hazlett, California State Department of Education, P.O. Box 944272, Sacramento, CA 94244-2720.

ISBN 0-8011-0760-1

CONTENTS

•

APPENDIXES

•

•

A MESSAGE FROM BILL HONIG
California Superintendent of Public Instruction

Several significant events provided the impetus for this little book. In Public Law 99-494, Congress designated 1987 as the Year of the Reader. The President of the United States issued a proclamation stating:

NOW, THEREFORE, I, RONALD REAGAN, President of the United States of America, do hereby proclaim the year of 1987 as the Year of the Reader, and I invite Governors of every State, employers, government officials, community leaders, librarians, members of the business community, publishers, school superintendents, principals, educators, students, parents, and all Americans to observe this year with appropriate educational activities to recognize the importance of restoring reading to a place of preeminence in our personal lives and in the life of our Nation.

California followed the lead of the Congress and the President by launching the California Reading Initiative and brought together many organizations to promote literacy. Community groups, parent clubs, and business leaders combined their talents to encourage programs of reading and writing for everyone. Many agencies—boards of education, governmental offices, and professional associations—published resolutions in support of the California Reading Initiative. The effect has been like that of a pebble thrown into the water, causing ripples throughout the state.

The National Reading Initiative extends the promotion of literacy across the nation. Parents, teachers, librarians, and individuals everywhere are renewing their efforts to bring children and books together. The ideas in *Celebrating the National Reading Initiative* come from near and far in a generous spirit of sharing among colleagues and friends. Readers are invited to explore these pages and to select from them the activities that they consider appropriate and enjoyable. The emphasis in this collection of activities is on celebrating the abundant gift that reading may bring to the lives of children and adults—one and all.

PREFACE

Celebrating the National Reading Initiative can help many parents fulfill a treasured dream: having their children become lifelong readers. The ability to read well is the keystone to children's success in school, for productive adult employment, and for realization of personal fulfillment.

Responding to the California Reading Initiative, parents, teachers, and librarians from throughout the country are working together to reduce illiteracy. The goals should be to eliminate illiteracy by preventing it and to develop a love of literature and of the wonder of words for each and every child.

Toward this end, in the spring of 1987, key people from across the nation formed a National Reading Initiative Coordinating Council to create the National Reading Initiative. This group discussed current research in reading, student interest and achievement in the subject, and the current state of curriculum and instruction, textbooks, testing, and teacher training. It also formulated a series of recommendations for the promotion of reading.

The first project of the Coordinating Council was the development of this publication, which highlights practices and activities that can be used to promote reading among preschoolers, school-age children, adolescents, and adults. The Coordinating Council's recommendations were shared with a working committee, whose task was to develop this document.

The working committee requested contributions from across the nation. Hundreds of suggested activities were received from friends of literacy. The working committee met monthly to read each contribution and to begin developing the document. The Coordinating Council received a draft document early in 1988 and approved a revised draft in March of that year.

In cooperation with the International Reading Association, other professional associations, county superintendents of schools, school districts, state offices of education, and institutions of higher education, the working committee is striving to make this book available to educators, colleagues, and friends of literacy. We extend our sincerest thanks to all of those connected with these efforts. You are helping to provide a lifelong gift to students, a love and appreciation for the values and joys of reading.

JAMES R. SMITH
Deputy Superintendent
Curriculum and Instructional Leadership Branch

TOMAS LOPEZ
Director
Office of Humanities Curriculum Services

FRANCIE ALEXANDER
Associate Superintendent
Curriculum, Instruction, and Assessment Division

ACKNOWLEDGMENTS

Hundreds of educators, librarians, and parents responded to California's invitation to share their ideas for promoting literacy; and they contributed generously to the treasure trove of suggestions and resources that appear on the pages of this book. Some of the materials we received were duplicates, and so we included only one of each; and we shortened many of the offerings to conserve space. However, we read each contribution with great care, and we are sincerely appreciative of all who responded so graciously. Our fondest hope, as we believe it is of each contributor, is that children will not only *learn to read* but also *will read* for a lifetime to gain intellectual growth and personal enjoyment.

We invite you to write to this book's contributors for additional information regarding their specific suggestions for promoting reading—celebrating a national interest in the written word.

The principal writers of this document were Janet McWilliams, Resource Teacher, Reading Program, San Juan Unified School District, Carmichael, California; Barbara Schmidt, Professor, Department of Teacher Education, California State University, Sacramento; and Eleanor Thonis, District Psychologist, Wheatland Elementary School District, Wheatland, California.

The cover illustration was prepared specially for this publication by James Marshall, noted writer and illustrator of children's books.

The overall processes and development were managed by Francie Alexander, Director, Curriculum, Instruction, and Assessment Division, California State Department of Education, and Janet Cole, Education Program Assistant, Office of Humanities Curriculum Services, California State Department of Education.

Finally, appreciation is extended to the National Reading Initiative Coordinating Council and to the staffs of the California State Department of Education's Bureau of Publications; Media Services Unit; English–Language Arts Unit, especially Shirley Hazlett and Donavan Merck; and the Office of Humanities Curriculum Services for their dedication in developing this exciting, innovative, and creative book.

NATIONAL READING INITIATIVE COORDINATING COUNCIL

Francie Alexander
Associate Superintendent
Curriculum, Instruction, and Assessment Division
California State Department of Education
Sacramento

Jane Berkowitz
President
JB Enterprises—New Directions in Education
Stamford, Connecticut

Maria Casillas-McGrath
Region Administrator, Operations
Region E
Los Angeles Unified School District

Bernice Cullinan
Professor of Early Childhood Education
New York University

Linda Davis
Deputy Superintendent
Division of Instruction
San Francisco Unified School District

Lenore Daw
District Librarian, K–12
Fresno Unified School District

J. Troy Earhart
Commissioner of Education
Providence, Rhode Island

LaVerne Gonzalez
San Jose State University
School of Humanities and the Arts

Margaret Mary Kimmel
Professor
School of Library and Information Science
University of Pittsburgh

Patricia S. Koppman
President, 1988-89
International Reading Association
San Diego

Beatrice LaPisto-Kirtley
Mayor Pro Tem
Bradbury, California

Margaret L. Lesher
Vice-President
Director of Community Services
Lesher Communications
Orinda, California

Priscilla Lynch
Educational Consultant
Brick, New Jersey

Janet Nielsen
Area Director, Bay Coastal Region
KQED Instructional Television
San Francisco

Jean Osborn
Associate Director
Center for the Study of Reading
University of Illinois
Champaign, Illinois

Diane Ravitch
Professor of History
Columbia University Teachers College
New York City

Barbara Schmidt
Professor
Department of Teacher Education
California State University, Sacramento

Raymond F. Sleater
Director, Book Service
National Office
Boy Scouts of America
Irving, Texas

Gary Strong
State Librarian
California State Library
Sacramento

Jim Trelease
Education Consultant
Reading Tree Productions
Springfield, Massachusetts

INTRODUCTION

Celebrating the National Reading Initiative is intended to challenge readers of all ages to celebrate the wonder of words arranged on the printed page. Everyone is invited to the celebration as the festivities burst forth in every direction:

- At home
- At school
- At the library
- Around the town
- Around the world

Each section of this book contains descriptions of activities that have been highly successful in drawing children into the golden circle of literacy and instrumental in keeping them there. Readers are urged to create their own versions of "Come to the Party" as they bring children and books together. The door prize is literacy!

You may have tangible wealth untold
Caskets of jewels and coffers of gold,
Richer than I you can never be —
I had a mother who read to me.

Strickland Gillilan
"The Reading Mother"

CELEBRATING AT HOME

READING ALOUD
•
GROWING A BOOKSTALK
•
TELL A BOOK
•
THE READING JAR
•
A GIFT IDEA
•
A PARTY IDEA
•
SCOUTS' SUGGESTIONS
•
A NEIGHBORHOOD BOOK
SHARE
•
FAMILY WRITING
•
FAMILY READING CONTEST
•
SUMMERTIME TIPS
•
PARENT INVOLVEMENT

PARENTS ARE THEIR CHILDREN'S FIRST TEACHERS. PARENTS REJOICE AS EACH MILESTONE is met and every skill is mastered. They find extraordinary pleasure in being an essential part of their children's development. During the preschool period and throughout the magical years of childhood, nothing gives parents greater satisfaction than watching their children gain literacy skills. Parents are essential partners in this exciting development.

When "Reading Aloud" to their children, parents offer more than the gift of the story. They give them warmth, safety, and love, which become strongly associated with stories and books. Memories of a father's voice or a mother's laughter are forever carried close to the heart. Children discover the wonder of words and probe the mystery of the world beyond their homes. They begin to experience the joy that books offer. They want to read, too, just as their parents read.

As parents and children read together, there is great excitement in watching their books grow in number and variety. They meet so many different characters and discover so many new places. Each book is a journey, and each story is an adventure. Each addition is accompanied by applause. "Growing a Bookstalk" is a delightful project which flourishes with the reader.

In a sense, children are books, too. Parents love to recount the unusual and clever things that their children have said. But how can parents begin to answer their questions? Do you know what the inside of a cloud looks like? Can your shadow get there before you do? What color is a burp? Parents may chronicle their children's bright and beautiful observations and may preserve these remarkable reflections as suggested in "Tell a Book."

During the vacation doldrums, families can continue to encourage language and literacy through incentives such as "The Reading Jar," which will tempt even the most indifferent reader to join the fun. Messages and treats are stored in this marvelous jar. The promise of boundless surprise draws the most reluctant readers to its mystical properties.

The gifts that parents choose for their children make memorable milestones of birthdays, promotions, and holidays. A suitable book is always a proper gift—the right size, the most becoming color, and the longest lasting remembrance for any occasion. No one ever says, "Don't buy a book, he has one!" If certain books can, for example, be combined with stuffed animals of their characters, the reward is doubled. "A Gift Idea" includes the how and who of such an activity.

Parties are grand for celebrating literature at home. Parents, neighbors, friends, and children can dress up as their favorite storybook people. All the guests are invited to have a good time and to live a splendid fantasy as they step from the pages of beloved books. "A Party Idea" gives directions for such a gala affair.

Neighborhood groups, the Boy Scouts and Girl Scouts, community clubs, and local reading councils can offer lively suggestions for bringing early readers along and for helping eager readers share their enthusiasm for books. "Scouts' Suggestions," "A Neighborhood Book Share," and "Summertime Tips" urge readers of all ages to rejoice in their own skills and to persuade others to come to the party.

Families can promote reading and writing in so many ways. Each family has its own traditions and rituals to mark the significant happenings of the home. Parents are models of literate behavior when they leave notes for their children and expect notes from them in return. Letters exchanged among extended family members are occasions for reading and writing. Lists of various household needs give importance to writing. "Family Writing" and "Family Reading Contest" suggest many ways of enticing young readers and writers to practice and perfect their crafts.

"Parent Involvement" outlines many practical ways in which parents can share in and increase the reading enjoyment of their children.

Families throughout the nation are asked to join in the celebration of language and literature. The festivities are taking place from coast to coast, and many of them are described on the following pages.

A good book is the best companion.

READING ALOUD

The national interest in reading to children flowered following the publication of *The Read-Aloud Handbook,* by Jim Trelease. Parents are urged to read aloud to their children often, beginning as early as infancy and continuing into adolescence. Some of the benefits to be realized from reading aloud are the following:

- Reading aloud to children helps children learn to read and contributes to their success in school. Reading anything at hand is useful—newspapers, road signs, labels, letters, and so on.
- Reading together builds a bond between parent and child.
- Reading by parents presents a model of behavior to be followed.
- Reading aloud is shared fun.

Contributed by
William F. Russell
Berkeley, California

GROWING A BOOKSTALK

As part of a project to encourage parents' and children's reading together, the Solano (California) County Reading Association designed a personal bookstalk, a chart for use by both children and parents titled "(child's name) and the Bookstalk." The leaves on the chart suggest the names of excellent books, and the chart itself serves as a stimulus and a record of literature shared by the parent and child.

The officers of the association recommend that the bookstalk be completed in this way:

- Color in the leaves on the stalk as the books are read and enjoyed.
- Add the names of other books on blank leaves.
- Write in the titles and authors of other favorite books.
- Read aloud to young children who are not yet able to read.
- Extend the height of the stalk as more books are discovered.

The growth chart serves as both a stimulus and an ongoing record of shared enjoyment of literature. As Betty Mendenhall and Kathy Raina, officers of the association, state, "The soothing sound of a mother's or father's voice reading a lyrical or descriptive passage to a child can have magical effects."

Contributed by
Barbara Schmidt, Professor
Department of Teacher Education
California State University
Sacramento

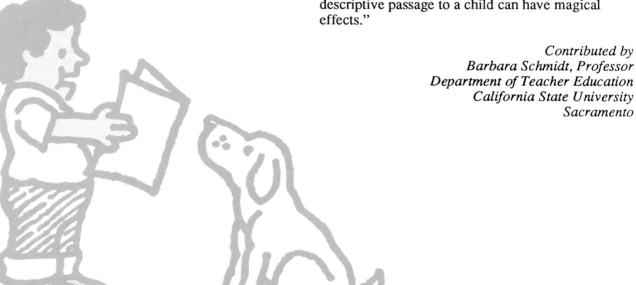

TELL A BOOK

Parents know that children say the most amazing things. Their first utterances may be poems in the making. One mother recorded her toddler's early attempts to create a haiku:

A tree
I take a bite.

And later,

The bumblebees
Are sleeping
In their bumblebeds.

To "tell a book," follow these simple steps:

- Get a wire-bound notebook and pen.
- Set aside 20 minutes each day for recording the child's storytelling. (Take the telephone off the hook.)
- Write verbatim the child's story as he or she tells it. (Be sure to avoid changing, adding, or rearranging. Keep the grammatical structures and invented words as they are given.)
- Read the story back to the child when it is finished.
- Read often from the notebook along with any other books in the child's library.
- Take pictures during the telling of the book.
- Collect several favorite stories, add the photos, and send the collection to the child's grandparents.

Contributed by
Carol L. Nyhoff
Berkeley, California

THE READING JAR

When children begin to read, their enthusiasm and skills are nurtured in school during the magic days of kindergarten and first grade. Alas! When summer comes, children are often caught up in other activities and may lose interest in reading. One very wise parent designed a "Reading Jar" as an incentive to keep children's skills alive and growing over the long summer months.

To make a "Reading Jar," follow these directions:

- Get a large clear plastic storage container with a screw-off lid.
- Fill the container with small wrapped treats— for example, bubble gum, peanuts, popcorn, and toys.
- Invite the child to take a treat from the jar after she or he reads to a member of the family.
- Keep the reading requirement short and within the child's abilities to complete.
- Increase the length of reading expected as the child's skills improve.
- Vary the contents of the jar to include notes, special privileges, and other age-appropriate incentives.

Contributed by
Maralee Karwoski
Yucaipa, California

A GIFT IDEA

Parents may introduce a major character in children's literature, using an exciting combination of a stuffed animal and a picture book that includes the animal. Some suggested animal characters are Peter Rabbit, Tom Kitten, Jemima Puddle-Duck, Paddington Bear, Curious George, Winnie-the-Pooh, Clifford the Big Red Dog, and Babar.

Parents should read the book to the child, and the parent and child should:

- Talk about the character.
- Pretend to be the character.
- Engage in play involving the character.

Contributed by
Janice Heirshberg
Los Angeles, California

A PARTY IDEA

Preschool-age children especially enjoy dressing up for a party. Favorite characters from children's literature are invited to the party. Parents, children, neighbors, and other party goers are included in the story party.

For a good time for one and all, here are some suggestions:

- Send invitations for guests to come dressed as favorite storybook characters.
- Remind the guests to bring the books in which their favorite characters are featured.
- Have a parade of the characters indoors or outdoors as the weather permits.
- Have games in which the characters must be identified from their costumes.
- Read the story, or a brief synopsis of the story, of each character.
- Conduct a treasure hunt with clues that lead to a chest filled with books.
- Give gift-wrapped books as prizes and party favors.
- Offer plenty of age-appropriate food, snacks, and drinks for the guests.

This activity may be adapted for children and adults of all ages. No one is ever too young or too old for the enchantment of a story party.

Contributed by
Susan Paradis, Teacher
Bristol, Connecticut

SCOUTS' SUGGESTIONS

The scouting groups to which many school-age children belong have many suggestions for encouraging beginning readers to practice their skills at home. Among their recommendations are these:

- Ask children to help in the preparation of a grocery list.
- Take them to the grocery store and have them find items on the list.
- Have them help to put away the groceries.
- Encourage the children to read the labels, the box tops, and the packages as they store them.
- Prepare a meal together and let them take needed items from shelves and storage areas.
- Have them read the ingredients from a recipe.
- Talk about the steps in preparing a meal—first, second, and so on.
- Elicit praise and appreciation from the family for the early reader who helped.

Contributed by
Mimi Hjersman, Director of Program Delivery
Tierra del Oro Girl Scouts
Rancho Cordova, California

Start a Ben Franklin Library Society:

- Ask everyone in the family to go on a weekend outing to the local library. Make sure each person has a valid library card.
- Ask a librarian to explain how the library is organized and how to use the card catalog. (Some modern libraries use microfiche or computer terminals.)
- Encourage each member of the family to check out a book that is of interest to her or him.
- On the following weekend bring family members together to share a snack and to take turns talking about the books they read. Then head to the library to return the books and check out others.
- Make this a weekly or monthly family activity; everyone could become as wise as Ben Franklin.

Contributed by
Raymond F. Sleater
Director, Book Service
National Office
Boy Scouts of America
Irving, Texas

A NEIGHBORHOOD BOOK SHARE

The connection between reading and life is strengthened by "A Neighborhood Book Share." The sharing takes place once a week at various homes in the community. The children gather to talk about the books they are reading, what they like or dislike about the books, and why they feel the way they do about them. The time is relatively unstructured, with children talking, and listening to others talk, about books. Their exchange is not *a school book report*; rather, it is a chance for them to express their opinions and to hear the opinions of others. The most important reason for getting together is to enjoy the camaraderie of a neighborhood literacy group.

The plan can be most successful when these few simple rules are followed:

- Limit the age span of the group to between two and three years.
- Include only the number of children that may fit comfortably in the homes in which the group will meet.
- Make every child feel successful, regardless of her or his reading skill.
- Emphasize the enjoyment of the occasion.
- Praise and encourage all the children for their efforts.
- Provide snacks and some free time for play.
- Keep the meeting short, approximately 1 hour.
- Make certain that everyone gets home safely.

If the "Neighborhood Book Share" idea catches on, more than one home may be opened on the sharing day or night, and various age groups of children may be invited to come to the home that hosts the appropriate age group.

Contributed by
Anne B. Seil
Petaluma, California

Ideas to encourage writing within the home come from many sources. Writing is intrinsically interesting to toddlers, who want to write even before they want to read.

Some suggestions for encouraging writing at home are the following:

- Appreciate every early attempt at writing. Praise writing efforts; make a fuss over them. At dinner, read whatever has been written.
- Display the writings on the refrigerator or a family bulletin board.
- Make copies of the writings and send them to the grandparents.
- Keep a scrapbook of funny incidents or favorite moments.
- Try writing poems, limericks, and stories as gifts for family members.
- Ask family members to contribute to letters that are to be sent to relatives.
- Have children enter writing contests.
- Write inscriptions in books that are given as gifts.

Contributed by
Anne V. Speyer
Pittsfield, Massachusetts

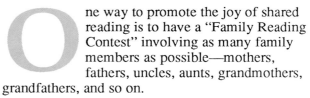

One way to promote the joy of shared reading is to have a "Family Reading Contest" involving as many family members as possible—mothers, fathers, uncles, aunts, grandmothers, grandfathers, and so on.

The rules of the contest may vary, but the basic guidelines are these:

At school

- Announce the name of the contest.
- Tell why the contest is being held.
- Identify the participants.
- Give the dates for the beginning and the end of the contest.
- Ask that some adult family member read to all those in the family who will listen.

At home

- Count the minutes that family members spend reading and listening.
- Write on a card the name of the book read and the time (in minutes) of each reading.
- Send the card to school once each week for the class to record the amount of time spent on reading and the names of the books that were read.

At regular intervals, winners should be announced in each class, and the classes which have the highest number of hours are given a party by the Parents' Club. Winners may be grouped by primary and intermediate classes.

Contributed by
The teaching staff of
Coyle Avenue Elementary School
San Juan Unified School District
Carmichael, California

Every book on parenting contains valuable hints on summertime play. Reading councils in several areas offer the following practical and reasonable tips for pleasurable summertime reading experiences:

- Read to children every day.
- Listen to children read every day if they know how to read.
- Find time to visit the library often with children.
- Encourage the retelling of stories.
- Write messages—plans, activities, and schedules of the day's events.
- Encourage children to respond in writing.
- Play word games—rhyming games, riddles, traveling games, and concentration-type games.
- Write children's personal words of interest on cards.
- Limit television time to what is deemed reasonable.
- Ask children to read the descriptions of their television programs from the newspaper or television guide.
- Share television watching with children occasionally.
- Discuss the content of a TV program after the program is over.
- Give books as gifts.

Contributed by
Stanislaus Reading Council
Stanislaus, California

Researchers who have investigated the effects of parental involvement on learning generally agree that parents contribute significantly to their children's achievement.

The following suggestions are intended to help engage parents in successful and long-lasting endeavors related to their children's school achievement:

- Be very clear about what is expected of parents.
- Make certain that the plan is comprehensive and reasonable.
- Provide the materials for all anticipated parent-child activities.
- Limit each activity to no more than a half hour.
- Send notes home emphasizing the importance of parents' reviewing their children's work.
- Use parent-orientation evenings to explain and promote involvement.
- Encourage responses from parents about assigned tasks.
- Express appreciation for the additional practice which parents provide.

Among the many benefits which accrue to students whose parents take an active part in their learning are these: Parents become aware of what is being covered in class, the students feel that their parents care about what they are learning, and school personnel sense the cooperative efforts of parents.

Contributed by
Grant Von Harrison
Brigham Young University
Salt Lake City, Utah

B was a Book
With a binding of blue,
And pictures and stories
For me and for you.
B
Nice little book!

Edward Lear

CHILDREN COME TO SCHOOL WITH THE EXPECTATION THAT THEY WILL LEARN TO READ and write. What a glorious place the school can be when it meets that expectation! Classrooms with book nooks, reading centers, poetry circles, and readers' clubs invite children to come to the literacy party, where everyone is celebrating reading. The school is a bright, cheerful place that beckons everyone to join the festival. Activities are planned to create interest in books—listening, talking, sharing, reading aloud, reading silently, and finding rewards. Print is found in books, magazines—everywhere. It is found on buttons, balloons, T-shirts, headbands, quilts, tickets, walls, and posters.

"The Reading Corner," created cooperatively by students, teachers, and reading experts, draws readers to its treasure much as a lodestone attracts iron ore. "The PAC Reader Program" enables older readers to realize their capabilities when they read regularly to younger children. In "A Reading Challenge," primary students are invited to compete in a reading marathon. The "Be Enthusiastic About Reading" (BEAR) program develops incentives for students and parents to put reading for pleasure high on their lists of out-of-school pursuits. "I Love to Wear Things I Can Read" encourages students to find interesting ways to put reading into their everyday lives. The "Readers' Club" involves a Battle of the Books competition to keep students reading year-round.

"Quilts and Burps" suggests making a quilt of squares representing books that children have read and describes a unique reading strategy for lunchtime called BURP (Bite of Uninterrupted Reading Program). The "Principal on the Roof" attracts great interest among students, parents, the community, and the media. The entire student body and staff are rewarded for their reading time by sending their principal to the roof for a day. The "Bookbusters—A Summer Reading Book Club" inspires students to include more reading time in their lives and to earn a T-shirt while doing so. "Sunrise School Reading Marathon" gives students the opportunity to trade their reading time for an overnight party. "The Royal Reader in the Classroom" provides a welcome complete with blaring trumpets and a jeweled crown for an invited guest deemed a Royal Reader. Students earn books in the "School-Home Reading Reward System." Journals about children's books and detailed suggestions to help in the classroom are found in "Ways to Use Magazines."

A system of classroom libraries integrated into the reading development program leads students to the acquisition of skills in listening, speaking, reading, writing, and thinking. The "Teaneck Reading Incentive Program" (TRIP) emphasizes literacy as a holistic process, one that is highly personal. "Welcome Words from West Virginia" describes the Book-It program, sponsored by Pizza Hut, and the television series "More Books from Cover to

Cover." Both the Book-It program and "More Books from Cover to Cover" interest students in reading more often and solicit their opinions in the selection of the best books for "The Children's Book Awards."

The "Women's Hall of Fame" is designed to create greater awareness of the contributions of women. The plan involves reading about the lives of prominent women, campaigning to have one's favorites included in the Hall of Fame, and presenting the choices to the rest of the school. The "Historical Fiction Projects" are planned to enhance the students' appreciation of the early American heritage. Students read some early textbooks, trace the famous trails to the West, recreate days in the lives of pioneers, and dramatize significant scenes from history.

"Spotlighting Readers and Writers" makes it possible for students to talk directly to the authors of books. The elaborate plan involves faculty, students, and administrators in a coordinated endeavor to call a specific author or to have a discussion of a particular book. The project is rooted in the beliefs that students of all reading levels can participate in the project and that the more children read, the better readers they become. "Reader's Theatre" offers an alternative to the wait-your-turn type of reading. It lends itself splendidly to cooperative learning and uses content from a variety of reading sources. The performers receive recognition and appreciation from their audience.

On "Poetry Day," students and teachers use an extended lunch hour to read favorite poems. The "Locked Closet Book Collection" is designed to stir the curiosity of students and to create enough mystery to make students wonder what may be in the books. "Students as Authors" publishes thousands of books and honors the student-authors at an awards ceremony to which the entire community is invited.

"Friday Night Prime Time" offers children a night out to read, see movies, talk, and eat together in a supervised setting. The evening may end at 11 p.m., or the children may stay over and enjoy Saturday breakfast. The experience has the promise of becoming a gala event. "Balloon Day" provides much excitement for students. They earn balloons for the books they have read, write tags on the balloons they have earned, and send the balloons up into the sky in a great ceremonial blast. The "Recite-a-Poem Contest" promotes the discovery and appreciation of poetry. Recitation takes place with great fanfare, complete with judges, prizes, and an appreciative audience.

These imaginative experiences in language and literacy are described in detail on the pages which follow. The nation is ablaze in a carnival of lights that beckon readers to renew their love affair with the beauty of words, to come to the feast of literature, and to discover the enchantment of books.

In reading, appetite is half the feast.

THE READING CORNER

The reading corner is a very special place in a classroom. It is filled with books, magazines, periodicals, newspapers, and student-authored materials. To create a reading corner, follow these suggestions:

- Ask the students to help in its creation.
- Follow simple guidelines for the selection of trade books.
- Include well-written materials chosen by both critics and students.
- Balance the choices between experts' and students' opinions.
- Stock the corner with a variety of print media. Use as many resources as possible.
- Keep the corner up to date, using advice from parents, students, and reading experts.
- Encourage daily use of the corner.
- Make the corner a source of information and pleasure.
- Organize the corner so that students can find things easily.

The creation of a reading corner is like the making of a sourdough mix: both processes are merely started and then left alone to grow. Hence, one watches the reading corner evolve from its modest beginnings to its fully grown state.

Contributed by
Lyndon Searfoss, Professor
Arizona State University
Tempe, Arizona

THE PAC READER PROGRAM

"The PAC Reader Program" stresses the advantages of peer learning. The program is designed to promote reading among younger students and to improve the self-image of older ones. Recently, one community honored 420 volunteer readers from the fifth and sixth grade classrooms.

A similar program in Alaska is called the "Adopt-a-Reader Education Merit Program."

To develop a "PAC Reader Program," follow these guidelines:

- Invite fifth and sixth grade students to volunteer to read to first and second graders.
- Include all students who wish to participate.
- Encourage students who are not great readers to join the group.
- Give volunteers training in how to select an appropriate book and how to read it aloud.
- Be sure the volunteers rehearse their reading with a teacher, an instructional aide, or a parent volunteer.

- Demonstrate how one introduces a book by giving the book's title and saying a few words about its author.
- Remind the readers to introduce themselves.
- Schedule the reading time so it is compatible with the school's routine.
- Allow for adequate preparation time between readings.
- Honor the "capable readers" in assemblies, at breakfasts, or at other school functions.

Contributed by
Cathy Lapsansky, Reading Supervisor
Terry McAndrew, Reading Specialist
Pittston Area School District
Yatesville-Pittston, Pennsylvania

Annie Calkins, Language Arts Specialist
Division of Educational Program Support
Alaska Department of Education
Juneau

Sue C. Hare, Superintendent
Lower Kuskokwim School District
Bethel, Alaska

Glen Rutherford, Principal
Chaptnguak Schools
Chefornak, Alaska

A READING CHALLENGE

A second grade teacher challenged all the second grade classes to celebrate the Year of the Reader. He placed an advertisement in the local newspaper and reported that over 500 students read over 10,000 books in a 50-day period. A copy of his challenge is shown below.

TEACHER'S READING CHALLENGE!

The 2nd grades at J.O. Ford School challenge all 2nd grade classes in the R.U.S.D. to a

READ-A-THON.

Celebrate the "Year of the Reader."

For more information, CALL BOB REPICKY

Contributed by
Nancy Whisler, Education Consultant
Sacramento, California

BE ENTHUSIASTIC ABOUT READING

Personnel from the "Be Enthusiastic About Reading" (BEAR) program in the Natick, Massachusetts, schools report nearly 100 percent participation among students in kindergarten through grade five. The program features active cooperation between parents and teachers to get students to read for pleasure during their leisure time.

The program's personnel recommend the following plan of action to develop a BEAR program:

- Send a letter to parents explaining the home-school incentive program. Include all the information that parents will need: the dates of the program, the number of minutes in a reading period, and parents' roles.
- Stress that the BEAR program is for enjoyment.
- Suggest ways parents and children can share books.
- Inform parents that the television set or radio should be turned off during reading periods.
- Refer parents to the school or local library for books that their children might enjoy.

Contributed by
N. Jerome Goldberg, Assistant Superintendent
Curriculum, Instruction, and Assessment
Natick Public Schools
Natick, Massachusetts

I LOVE TO WEAR THINGS I CAN READ

A fourth grade teacher at Sonoma Elementary School, Battle Creek, Michigan, promoted a week-long celebration of reading in her "I Love to Wear Things I Can Read" program.

The activities for each day are scheduled as follows:

- Monday: Reading Jogs the Mind—Children wear jogging clothes, including running shoes.
- Tuesday: Button Day—Children wear buttons with words on them and/or design their own buttons with words.
- Wednesday: T-shirt or Sweatshirt Day—Children wear T-shirts or sweatshirts with writing on them. They may also wear shirts with the names of faraway places on them, locate the places on maps, and talk about them.
- Thursday: Hat and Headband Day—Children wear hats or headbands with names, insignia, or sayings on them; modify hats to make them represent characters in books; and/or design logos or insignia for hats and headbands.
- Friday: Book Day—Children identify favorite books, write the titles and names of the authors on cards, and then "wear" their favorite books (pin the cards on their clothing).

Contributed by
James L. Newnum, Elementary
Reading Consultant
Harper Creek Community Schools
Battle Creek, Michigan

READERS' CLUB

A "Quiz Bowl" type of competition in reading can stimulate the development of students' skills in listening, speaking, reading, and writing.

To organize a "Readers' Club," do the following:

- Prepare a videotape or slide show that describes a Battle of the Books.
- Compile a book list to be sent home with report cards.
- Plan with the school and community librarians to have the listed books on reserve shelves.
- Encourage students to read the books on the list. Make certain that teachers also read them. Write questions of different levels of difficulty from at least 50 books for use in the Battle of the Books.
- Arrange grade-level competitions to select finalists from each participating school.
- Choose a date for the finalists from each grade level of each school to compete.
- Appoint judges (preferably teachers and librarians) and a moderator to ask the questions about the books.
- Invite parents and community members to attend the Battle.
- Encourage local bookstores to donate books for prizes.
- Serve refreshments.
- Give everyone who has read at least ten books a certificate of recognition.
- Announce the winners—the students who, in the judges' opinion, answered the most questions correctly.
- Solicit coverage from the news media to recognize not only the winners but also all of the participants.

Contributed by
Ida May Sonntag, Department Chairperson
Fort Miami School
Maumee, Ohio

QUILTS AND BURPS

A reading teacher in Richmond, California, has her students contribute to a literature quilt. The quilt is made after many stories have been heard and read.

To make such a quilt:

- Ask each student to select a book to be remembered in the quilt.
- Create a square that contains something of interest in the book.
- Make the square as attractive and recognizable as possible.
- Put all the squares together to complete the quilt.
- Finish the quilt with the necessary quilting, binding, and background.
- Use the quilt to promote additional discussions of the books.
- Allow the students to take turns taking the quilt home to share with their families and friends.

A principal in the same school district started the "Bite of Uninterrupted Reading Program" (BURP). The program takes place three days a week during the lunch period.

To develop a BURP:

- Prepare tickets for students' admission to the readings.
- Give each teacher two tickets for distribution to students of the teacher's choice.
- Recruit parents, speech therapists, and central office staff to do the oral reading.
- Select the books to be used.
- Divide the read-aloud sessions into groups of primary and intermediate students.
- Admit the students with tickets to the read-aloud sessions during the last half of the lunch hour.

Contributed by
Nancy Whisler, Education Consultant
Sacramento, California

PRINCIPAL ON THE ROOF

An elementary school principal in San Gabriel, California, offered to spend a whole school day on the school's roof if the students met a challenge to read for 60,000 minutes outside their classes. Each of the 635 students in kindergarten through grade six had to read 10 minutes at home every night to put the principal on the roof.

Below are the simple procedures for putting any principal on the roof:

- Prepare a weekly home reading form to record the number of minutes students read at home.
- Remind parents to sign the forms and to return them each week.
- Ask the teachers to total weekly the number of minutes of reading time for each student.
- Total the number of minutes the class has read.
- Record the minutes on a class chart.
- Submit the totals to the principal's office.
- Post the class totals on a schoolwide chart and display the chart in a prominent place in the school.
- Decide on a reasonable time period for the students to try to meet the principal's challenge.
- Encourage older students who have met their goals to help younger ones.
- Place a desk, telephone, and other necessities on the roof so that the principal can continue her or his work for the designated day.
- Arrange times for the different classes to see the principal at work on the roof.
- Invite the media to cover the extraordinary sight of the principal on the roof.

Contributed by
Susan S. Crum, Principal
McKinley Elementary School
San Gabriel Elementary School District
San Gabriel, California

BOOKBUSTERS—A SUMMER READING BOOK CLUB

The staff of Johnson Park Elementary School in Olivehurst, California, planned a reading program, "Bookbusters," to promote reading over the summer months. Specifically, the staff wanted to promote the following:

- Reading for pleasure
- Using the library
- Improving attitudes toward reading
- Increasing reading comprehension and fluency
- Encouraging families to read together

Here are some suggestions to organize and carry out such a program:

- Tell the students that the primary requirement is for participants to read 50 books during the summer vacation.
- Inform students of the possible prizes: T-shirts, paperback books, and so on.
- Provide a list of suitable books.
- Send home information relative to the bookmobile's schedule, library hours, and other useful data.
- Remind the younger students that being *read to* counts for them.
- Include some reading games in a packet to be sent home with the students.
- Prepare a simple form for the students to use to record the books they read.
- Schedule parent volunteers, teachers, and teachers' aides to staff the library during designated hours.
- Report on the readers and their successes when school opens in the fall.
- Encourage the wearing of Bookbusters T-shirts.

Contributed by
The teaching staff of
Johnson Park Elementary School
Marysville Joint Unified School District
Marysville, California

SUNRISE SCHOOL READING MARATHON

The "Sunrise School Reading Marathon" was devised as a method of improving students' reading skills and increasing their reading pleasure. The period from July 25 through October 18 was set aside for the marathon. The expected goal was a minimum of 2,000 hours of reading, and the reward for students who reached the goal was an overnight party at Sunrise School.

To set the reading marathon in motion, do the following:

- Announce the dates for the marathon.
- Clarify the rules of the marathon.
- Notify the parents of their roles and their contributions.

- Prepare cards to record the number of minutes students read.
- Encourage the parents to read at the same time that their children do and in a quiet, family setting.
- Tell the students that their reading times will be recorded on a master chart.
- Post the recorded data in the school's multipurpose room.
- Arrange a party and invite the winners.

Contributed by
Mary Mastain, Reading Specialist
San Juan Unified School District
Carmichael, California

Beverley Hendrickson, Principal
Dewey Fundamental School
San Juan Unified School District
Carmichael, California

THE ROYAL READER IN THE CLASSROOM

Each Friday morning is Royal Reader time in Cynthia Sather's fourth grade class at Woodside School in the San Juan Unified School District, Carmichael, California. At precisely 10:30, the red carpet is unfurled, the throne—a high-backed, gilt-painted, oak chair—is readied, and a welcoming committee greets the invited guest with a red-velvet cape and jeweled crown. To the blare of trumpets (on an audiocassette), the honored guest is led to the throne past a cheering, clapping phalanx of enthusiastic fourth graders.

Ms. Sather instituted Royal Reader Day several years ago after hearing about it in a workshop. She says that the event has encouraged her students to *want* to read quality material more than ever.

Listed below are the steps to be followed:

- Nominate possible guests early in the school year. Have the students suggest the nominees.
- Allow students to take the role of host.
- Have the students compose letters and send them to the invited guests.
- Ask the guests to bring the books they are reading at the time or to bring their favorite children's books.
- Request that the guests respond (RSVP) to the class's invitation.

The class has invited as Royal Readers the mayor, a local TV anchorperson, a member of a professional basketball team, several grandmothers, a bus driver, the school's custodian, and an ex-astronaut. (The principal was somewhat miffed that he was not invited until May.)

Contributed by
Barbara Schmidt, Professor
Department of Teacher Education
California State University, Sacramento

SCHOOL-HOME READING REWARD SYSTEM

The "School-Home Reading Reward System" offers books as rewards for students' reading a specified number of hours at home. The following quotas, by grade level, are used:

Kindergarten—6 hours
First grade—8 hours
Second grade—10 hours
Third grade—12 hours
Fourth grade—14 hours
Fifth grade—16 hours

The program is successful because of the cooperative efforts of teachers, students, parents, and the school librarian.

To implement a "School-Home Reading Reward System":

- In a letter or newsletter, send a description of the program to parents. Include all necessary information—a tally sheet on which to record the hours students read, parents' roles, and verification of the reading that has been done. The data should be returned to the teacher.
- Specify the rewards—books of the students' choice, a maximum of two books a month.
- Record the home reading times on a master chart for each classroom.
- Recognize the readers at each grade level at school assemblies.
- Reward teachers with books of their choice.
- Publicize the "super-duper readers" on the school's bulletin board.
- Encourage local bookstores to provide gift certificates and books.

The children get "hooked" on reading for the enjoyment it provides. Of a total enrollment of 392 students, 356 have earned at least one book. The top students have earned as many as 21 books. The program is achieving the objectives set by the teachers and parents.

Contributed by
Barbara Garrop, Project Director
Mills Elementary School
Benicia Unified School District
Benicia, California

WAYS TO USE MAGAZINES

Teachers can discover dozens of surprising stories about books in *The Horn Book Magazine.* These stories can bring books and authors alive in the classroom. The magazine is a comprehensive journal of children's books and contains articles by authors, illustrators, and critics.

Teachers can learn how certain books came to be written and why they are important to readers of today and those of future generations. In an extensive book review section, teachers can become aware of the very best books being published today for young people. Columns by teachers, booksellers, publishers, and other writers approach children's literature from every different professional perspective and give educators the opportunity to apply ideas from other fields of interest.

The magazine also has news and information about recent awards and prizes, upcoming conferences, and relevant events in the world of books.

Teachers who are knowledgeable about children's books are the "best friends" that students can have. Such teachers can help students develop the reading and writing skills that are crucial to future success; they can also open up a world of adventure and a lifetime of pleasure.

Ways to use a comprehensive journal like *The Horn Book Magazine* are described below:

- Write a program. Students can report on their own literary activities in much the same way that columnists report on "Books in the Classroom" or that other writers provide the brief pieces that are often featured in "Hunt Breakfast" in *The Horn Book Magazine.* When the students' essays are completed, they can be submitted for inclusion in the school's PTA bulletin or student newspaper or even to the local paper for possible publication.
- Create a reviewer. Book reviews can help children grasp for themselves the fundamentals of reviewing a book. Teachers should start calling book reports book reviews and help their students shape their reviews with examples from the magazine.

- Create an advertising copywriter. Instead of a book report or book review, introduce advertising copywriting about books by having students study ads and then write their own copy about the books they have just read.
- Create an advertisement. Follow the copywriting sessions with sessions on advertising design. Students will have to choose an illustration, write blurbs, and select or invent quotes from other review journals. They will then attempt to arrange all these diverse elements in a pleasing ad.
- Write a second look. A standard feature is a look back at a previously published book the critic has known about for some time but has not looked at for a while. Have students list some of their preschool and kindergarten favorites—for example, *Curious George* or *Make Way for Ducklings*—and then write about them from their current, more mature perspective.
- Grab a book review. Clip from back issues reviews of books that are appropriate for students and place the reviews in a shoe box. When students need new books to read, send them to the shoe box to make an appropriate selection.
- Grab an author. Clip whole articles about an author or illustrator. When the time comes for a report or a special project, send students to the grab-box for a subject of interest.
- Turn students into "booktalkers." Older children who enjoy books can be encouraged to introduce good books to younger children. They select interesting picture-book reviews and visit classrooms with the books to talk about them.

Teachers can promote this project with the grab-box of reviews, combine it with the students' new review-writing skills and library skills, and encourage the connection between reading books, writing about them, and talking about them.
- Publish a class journal or magazine. A classroom full of readers can create its own review journal by developing a format and structure suitable to the children's age level. Children will have to work together and use all they have learned throughout the year about their favorite books and authors.

Contributed by
Amy L. Cohn, Marketing Manager
The Horn Book, Inc.
Boston, Massachusetts

TEANECK READING INCENTIVE PROGRAM

The "Teaneck Reading Incentive Program" (TRIP) is planned to draw on the experiences, abilities, and preferences of students. During the summer, teachers read a variety of reading materials intended to appeal to the different interests of students. A significant outcome of the teachers' summer efforts is their creation of classroom libraries.

The Teaneck Reading Incentive Program can be implemented as follows:

- Select books which can be integrated in a developmental reading program.
- Choose some books which correlate with specific grade-level reading activities.
- Add books which offer extensions of important skills.
- Provide students time for personal selection and reading.
- Design activities to integrate reading skills in other aspects of the curriculum.
- Emphasize critical and creative thinking about what has been read.
- Encourage the creation of ideas through words and pictures.
- Have students share reading by working in pairs.
- Keep records in some simple form.
- Establish a DEAR (Drop Everything and Read) time and have students enjoy the classroom libraries.

- Use wall charts, index cards, and individual records to keep track of students' interests and progress.
- Display students' work on bulletin boards and "bookworms" and in reading logs and folders.
- Encourage discussions of books among students.
- Develop additional strategies which go beyond traditional book reports—a television miniseries or a television guide entry, a book advertisement, or crossword puzzles of characters from books.

The classroom libraries foster a love for reading and an incentive to read. It is reasonable to predict that classroom libraries will also have a great potential for improving students' reading comprehension and critical thinking. Moreover, the "Teaneck Reading Incentive Program" has students rejoicing in their very own literacy.

Contributed by
John E. Cowen, Director
Office of Curriculum and Instruction
Flory Perini, Language Arts Supervisor
Teaneck Public Schools
Teaneck, New Jersey

WELCOME WORDS FROM WEST VIRGINIA

In West Virginia schools, teachers stimulate an interest in books with several enticing activities designed to celebrate the rewards of reading. Among their most successful efforts are these:

- An instructional television series, "More Books from Cover to Cover," introduces exceptional books. Each 15-minute program presents a story without an ending. To finish the story, students must find the books at their libraries.
- The Book-It program, sponsored by a local Pizza Hut, rewards students with free personal-size pizzas for the books that they have read. The classroom teacher records the number of books read and distributes the certificates to qualifying students each month.
- The "Children's Book Awards" is a program in which students review books and vote for their favorites. When the winning book and two other honor books are selected, the students participate in a day of celebration at West Virginia State University. They attend storytelling sessions, puppet shows, plays, folk music presentations, and art displays. Best of all, perhaps, they hear the author of the winning book as the guest speaker.
- A public television program is sent to all schools in the state so that many students can listen to the author whose work is being honored.

Contributed by
Karen Simon, Coordinator
English/Language Arts, Reading
West Virginia Department of Education
Charleston

WOMEN'S HALL OF FAME

Memorial Boulevard Junior High School in Bristol, Connecticut, promotes a campaign for inducting notable women into a "Women's Hall of Fame." The school has a practical plan, which coincides with Women's History Week in March.

A successful campaign can be carried out as follows:

- Explain the purpose of the campaign to the students.
- Make available to the students autobiographies and biographies of notable women.
- Ask the students to select and read one of the autobiographies or biographies.
- Have the students prepare a short (6- to 8-minute) speech on behalf of their candidate for the Hall of Fame.
- Ask the students to provide slogans, posters, pamphlets, buttons, or balloons endorsing their candidates.
- Arrange a date for the voting and obtain a ballot box, voting sheets, and banners for the day of the voting.
- Announce the winner and plan an installation ceremony.
- Invite parents and other guests, including the press, to the event.
- Make the "Women's Hall of Fame" an annual affair.

Contributed by
Darlene B. Lefevre
Memorial Boulevard Junior High School
Bristol, Connecticut

HISTORICAL FICTION PROJECTS

The past comes alive as students think about how people traveled and lived in other times and places. Using historical fact and fiction as sources, encourage students to do some of the following:

- Display early textbooks—*New England Primer*, *McGuffy Readers*, and *The Hornbook of Virginia History*.
- Read from collections of maxims and proverbs—for example, *A Gathering of Days: A New England Girl's Journal, 1830–1832*, by Joan W. Blos.
- Recreate a pioneer school day with students writing on slates, reciting poems, competing in spelling bees, and singing the multiplication tables.
- Organize centers for pioneer activities— weaving, candle making, carding and spinning wool, quilting, cooking, making butter, playing pioneer games, singing, and dancing.
- Make a time line of important events described in the class's history book.
- Trace famous American trails on a map of the United States. Mark the routes taken by pioneers in books of fiction—for example, *On to Oregon*, by Honore Morrow, and the *Little House Books*, by Laura Ingalls Wilder.
- Write an advertisement convincing people to come to America.
- Write an advertisement persuading people to move to the West.
- Illustrate important events from a story or book.
- Dramatize historical scenes from books.
- Make a historical quilt.
- Play the role of a reporter from an eastern newspaper and report on life on the frontier.
- Display the means of transportation—steam locomotive, wagon train, and horse and buggy—from certain periods.
- Keep a journal that might have been written by a fictional historical character or a real figure from another era.

Contributed by
Kathleen L. Miller
Sally K. Ride Elementary School
The Woodlands, Texas

SPOTLIGHTING READERS AND WRITERS

Many readers and writers in South Carolina have been helped to find reading rewards through the ingenious use of the telephone in their reading programs. A quest for a more enthusiastic response to books from 1,000 junior high school students led to arrangements that enabled students to talk directly with authors by telephone. The excitement has kept the students searching, asking questions, and reading.

To make the student-author conversations possible:

- Prepare carefully in advance for the conversations, using the talents of faculty and students.
- Rent a conference telephone set from the local phone company and arrange to cover the costs of the rental and the long-distance call. Limit the interviews to 24 minutes.
- Write to the author's publisher to ask for an interview.
- Make the author's book or books available.
- Assign reading to students.
- Allow sufficient lead time for reading and discussion before conducting the telephone interview.
- Encourage class discussion of the theme, plot, characters, and style.
- Ask the students to prepare questions for the interview. Screen the questions to avoid duplicates.
- Develop follow-up activities to keep students' interest alive.
- Be certain to involve *all* students—not just the good readers.

J. Floyd Hall, Superintendent of the School District of Greenville County, states that the reading levels of the students have improved significantly as a result of their involvement in this program.

Contributed by
Pat Scales, Media Specialist
Greenville Middle School
The School District of Greenville County
Greenville, South Carolina

POETRY DAY

A standing-room-only crowd participates in "Poetry Day" in Torrance, California. Poetry readings are given in the library by teachers who read their favorite poems to the students. The activity is arranged by extending the lunch hour. Both the students and staff are invited to listen.

To organize a poetry day, follow these recommendations:

- Extend the lunch hour of the entire school for a reasonable period of time.
- Publicize "Poetry Day" on posters, in bulletins, and in memos.
- Invite faculty members to read their favorite poems.
- Arrange the library or any other comfortable area of the school for the readings.
- Provide appropriate seating by supplying such items as chairs, pillows, or rugs. Also, provide a microphone for the readers.
- At subsequent meetings, encourage the students to read their favorite poems.

Contributed by
Richard Moore, Librarian
Torrance High School
Torrance Unified School District
Torrance, California

READER'S THEATRE

A s an alternative to round-robin reading, "Reader's Theatre" offers every student in class an opportunity to take part in a dramatization. Students may be performers, stagehands, narrators, or audience members. Everyone is successful in one assigned role or another.

To conduct a "Reader's Theatre," follow these suggestions:

- Select a suitable text (fiction or nonfiction) and create dialogues from the material.
- Assign parts and distribute the script among the students.
- Prepare the students for the vocabulary by providing word cards for practice at home.
- Arrange for the narrators to describe the setting, present the scene, or introduce the background for the story.
- Discuss, before and after the presentation, the story plot, the characters, and the events.
- Encourage the students to practice reading aloud at home and with a partner at school.
- Stretch the imaginations of the audience members—have them picture in their minds the characters and the action.
- Select simple, easy-to-obtain props if they can enhance the meaning and enjoyment of the story.
- Consider having students write their own scripts from material that interests them.
- Repeat the performances for a variety of audiences—classmates, parents, younger students, other classes, or the total school.

The success of "Reader's Theatre" is largely attributable to the chance for students to "own" the materials, work as a group, make decisions, and express personal preferences. The "Reader's Theatre" is an enjoyable experience for all those involved.

Contributed by
Adrienne Stecher, Teacher
North Sacramento Elementary School District
Sacramento, California

LOCKED CLOSET BOOK COLLECTION

The "Locked Closet Book Collection" offers intrigue and mystery to arouse the interest of reluctant readers. During an assigned or free reading period, students are invited to select books from the locked closet. The contents are carefully shrouded in mystery and may be taken from the closet only when the teacher unlocks the door. Students are then free to choose from among the treasures of the closet—award-winning books, books nominated for the California Young Reader Medal, and other outstanding selections. There is great satisfaction in students' expressing the personal reward of reading a *whole book* for the first time.

Assemble a locked closet as follows:

- Choose titles from lists of favorite books, those most frequently read by young adults.
- Have no more than five copies of any one title.
- Put only paperback books in the closet.
- Read all the books in the closet yourself before giving them to students.
- Begin with a small number of books and add about three new titles each year.
- Keep the records simple—a single sign-up sheet on the inside of the closet door is sufficient.
- Encourage discussion and sharing of the books with others who have read them.
- Keep the closet locked unless students request to see its contents.

Contributed by
Gail Long, Chair
English Department
Leigh High School
Campbell Union High School District
San Jose, California

STUDENTS AS AUTHORS

"Students as Authors" involves 53 schools and thousands of student authors. On a designated conference day, schools are responsible for setting up displays of published books. The students share their ideas, browse through books, and participate in related activities—calligraphy, puppetry, story-telling, and poetry writing. The authors receive awards at a ceremony to which parents and community members are invited.

To get students writing and publishing, follow these suggestions:

- Provide information to teachers and parents.
- Encourage teachers to promote original writings as class projects.
- Assist students in revising and editing their writing.
- Arrange to have a final editorial review.
- Publish and bind the student-authored books.
- Plan a ceremony which involves students, parents, and community members. Make the ceremony a memorable event in which students are honored.
- Award certificates and other prizes as available.
- Place the student-authored books in school and classroom libraries for continued enjoyment.

Contributed by
Evelyn Friedman
Los Angeles Unified School District
Region H
Los Angeles, California

AUTHOR/ILLUSTRATOR DAY

An "Author/Illustrator Day" is a reading motivation program designed to promote students' enjoyment of reading. The time allotment involved depends on a commitment from the school district librarian. The total cost will vary, depending on the costs of travel, lodging, meals, and so on.

The following are suggestions for planning an author/illustrator visit:

- Determine which author/illustrator the students would like to have visit the school.
- Determine a funding source from which to cover the various costs of the program. The costs of honoraria, lodging, and meals should be considered. Possible funding sources include the PTA and student body funds and moneys from special programs.
- Decide which staff member(s) will coordinate and implement "Author/Illustrator Day" and delegate the responsibilities to the different staff members.
- Present "Author/Illustrator Day" to the staff with suggestions for implementation.
- Coordinate activities and duties with the district librarian.

For more detailed information, see Appendix A.

Contributed by
Janet McWilliams, Reading/Language Arts Resource Teacher
San Juan Unified School District
Carmichael, California

FRIDAY NIGHT PRIME TIME

The creation of lifelong readers is the primary reason for "Friday Night Prime Time." The plan is designed to bring adults and children together to celebrate the love of reading. "Friday Night Prime Time" begins in the early evening on Friday and ends on Saturday morning. Students talk, eat, sing, play, snack, see movies, listen to stories, and *read*. Two variations of "Prime Time" are (1) a sleep-over; and (2) an evening program that ends around 11 p.m.

"Friday Night Prime Time" is organized as follows:

- Describe the plan to parents, staff, and students—its purposes, arrangements, and details.
- Obtain permission from parents for the children to participate.
- Ask students to come with brown-bag dinners, pillows, stuffed animals, sleeping bags, and *books*.
- Plan activities to engage students' interest.
- Arrange for adult supervision.
- Organize breakfast if the overnight alternative is selected.
- Provide for award certificates to be distributed at the end of the activity.

Contributed by
R. Jean Carlin, Reading Coordinator
Elementary Division
D. C. Heath and Company
Novato, California

Jean Dunham, Principal
Pine Grove Elementary School
Orcutt Union Elementary School District
Orcutt, California

Barbara Hanno, Reading Product Manager
Elementary Division
D. C. Heath and Company
Lexington, Massachusetts

BALLOON DAY

"Balloon Day" is a reading incentive program with a goal of having students become more involved in reading for pleasure. The program covers a span of approximately two months. The cost is approximately $250 to $350.

To hold a "Balloon Day," follow the steps outlined below. Each step includes suggested materials for this project.

- Present pertinent information to the staff.
- Establish the criteria for students to earn balloons.
- Set up a "Balloon Day" Committee. Some schools use teachers, media technicians, PTA members, and parent volunteers. The number of committee members needed will depend on your school's population.
- Contract with a company to have a hot-air balloon visit on "Balloon Day."
- Present weather balloons to the classes in which 100 percent of the students earned balloons.
- Encourage parents to read with the students and also earn balloons.
- Have staff prepare a thank-you luncheon or some other activity of appreciation for all the parent volunteers and helpers.

For additional information, see appendixes B through G.

Contributed by
Janice Moore, Principal
Fair Oaks Elementary School
Penny Schott, Peck Elementary School
San Juan Unified School District
Carmichael, California

RECITE-A-POEM CONTEST

The "Recite-a-Poem Contest" is used to promote children's discovery and appreciation of poetry. Research is showing that memorizing is an exercise for the brain. The more exercise one does, the better one is at that activity. The cost of this contest is approximately $85. The time required is three to four weeks.

The following steps should be followed to help present such a program at individual school sites:

- Establish guidelines for the selection of students and poetry.
- Present the "Recite-a-Poem Contest" to the staff.
- Encourage staff and parents to volunteer as "Recite-a-Poem" committee members and assign tasks to the committee members.

For additional details about the "Recite-a-Poem Contest," see appendixes H through L.

Contributed by
Janet McWilliams
Reading/Language Arts Resource Teacher
San Juan Unified School District
Carmichael, California

Books to the ceiling, books to the sky.
My piles of books are a mile high.
How I love them!
How I need them!
I'll have a long beard by the time
I read them.

Arnold Lobel

CELEBRATING IN THE LIBRARY

THE LIBRARY IS A QUIET, SAFE PLACE. IT IS COMFORTABLE, COZY, AND WARM. Books stand at attention on their shelves. Chairs and tables arranged in convenient corners bid the patrons welcome. Pictures, posters, book jackets, and art objects tell the wordless stories of other lands, other people, and other times. The library is an inviting place. Its neat and tidy ambience is often a refuge in a disorganized and untidy world. The patrons and staff talking in muted tones offer a welcome contrast to the strident voices outside the library's protective walls. Children who discover the joys of the library visit again and again to discover new feelings and to experience undreamed of adventures. Librarians everywhere are urged to raise their voices as the National Reading Initiative is celebrated. Shout and be glad for the great gift of libraries wherever they are found. Raise those soft voices in songs and cheers for libraries. The literacy party could not take place without them.

In one community the central location of the library and its close proximity to the elementary schools, junior high, and high school make possible a natural partnership between the library and the schools. This "Partnership—School and Public Library" keeps the celebration of literacy going all year. First grade students have the very real expectation that learning to read and reading to learn is what school is all about. The "First Grade Roundup" keeps such an expectation alive and growing in many enjoyable activities to make the library a vital part of the first grader's reading.

"Books and Birthdays" encourages the students to discover the delights in the library and to share their pleasure with others. In another community, "A Family–Public Library Read-Aloud" has created considerable excitement among library patrons. This creative outreach to children and their families has spread, like ripples caused by a pebble thrown into a pond, to other libraries.

"Book Buddies and More" carries a message of cheer to many children for whom the library may not be part of their realities. Boys and girls in hospitals, students for whom English is not the native language, and children whose parents are unfamiliar with libraries are drawn to the enchanted circle of story times, video productions, and talking books. In "Books on the Move," the library comes to the students as librarians visit classrooms to talk about books, and the local bookmobile rolls along after school to bring a world of wonder to latch-key children. In "Inside and Outside a Book," students are treated to a different display each month as various countries are featured in selected books. The librarian writes, "We try to make our library warm and cozy, like a good book."

In another community, the teachers and librarians have organized "The Battle of the Books," a competition that includes complete rules and prizes for finalists. Champion readers are recognized and appreciated for their special love of books as well as for their prowess during "battle." The taste of victory and the joy of winning carry on throughout the year in listening, speaking, reading, and writing activities.

"Color Coding" offers a reasonable alternative to reading for adults who may not be functionally literate. A variety of nonprint media—videotapes, audiotapes, films, and computer software—make a rich storehouse of appealing genres accessible to library patrons. The materials are color-coded for ease of selection and management. In "The Endless Chain of Reading," library books are promoted for a 30-day period. As students complete their readings, they make paper chains that are linked together in a progressive reading chain to adorn the school's media center. The chains are then brought to the central office, where one endless chain of reading is ceremoniously festooned around the room amid applause and congratulations.

In "A Readers' Group for High School," readers are enticed to take part in before-school activities in which books are shared and enjoyed. Included are planned opportunities for high school students to read to elementary schoolchildren. Although students are accustomed to competition of all kinds, such as sports events, talent searches, quiz shows, and games of chance, they find the "Readers' Group" challenge very unusual.

Librarians are the gatekeepers of a depository of beauty, truth, enchantment, and wisdom that is available for a smile and a song. Even for readers who fail to smile or who are not of very good voice, the library and its treasures call.

PARTNERSHIP—SCHOOL AND PUBLIC LIBRARY

Grandview Heights, Ohio, is singularly blessed in the location of its public library, which is close to elementary schools, the junior high, and the high school. A happy proximity promotes a variety of jointly sponsored school-library activities to bring students closer to books and to nonprint media. Some of the partnership ventures are the following:

- Elementary school students visit the library in class groups to hear stories, see special programs, or check out books.
- Teachers draw on the extensive film library to borrow films for viewing in class.
- Teachers also take their classes to the library for films and follow-up activities with books and other resources.
- Children in special categorical groups visit the library on a regular basis.
- High school students come to the library to work on research projects.
- The library's staff members visit the schools to attend special events, to bring news of special programs, or to read to the students in their classrooms.
- The library frequently changes its opening hour to accommodate early visitors.
- Library personnel often attend evening open houses and back-to-school nights.
- Library representatives arrange for a table to give out applications for library cards and other information.
- The library's staff members select and disseminate reading material on parenting and on problems of adolescents.
- The children's section librarian often attends parent-teacher organization meetings to display award-winning literature.
- The library's staff members extend the facility's hours for teachers as needed.
- The classroom teachers can call on the librarians' expertise to gather a suitable collection of books on a specific topic.
- The schools and the library cooperate on community programs outside the schools—for example, festivals for a booster club or band concerts presented by the junior and senior high schools.

- The schools offer their facilities when the library needs additional space for special events—puppet shows, candidates' night, and so on.
- The library serves as the collection center for school redeemables.
- The school and library share an experienced teacher as a liaison and consultant.
- The liaison assists in distributing fliers, displaying posters, and suggesting recipients of the library's book give-aways.
- The staffs of both the school and the library remind students when their library cards need to be renewed.
- The liaison serves on various committees in the community to exchange ideas and to add to her or his professional knowledge.

The cooperative efforts of the school and the library personnel promote a shared commitment which inspires a love of literature. The joint investment between the community and the library increases the quality of life for all those involved.

Contributed by
T. Michael Weddle
Thomas A. Edison Elementary School
Grandview Heights City Schools
Columbus, Ohio

FIRST GRADE ROUNDUP

"First Grade Roundup" in the Kent County (Michigan) Library System has generated nationwide interest. Invitations to the program are sent to every elementary school in the service area, and virtually every first grade child attends the library program and receives a library card.

"First Grade Roundup" is carried out as follows:

- The members of the library staff are introduced to the children.
- The staff members present theater excerpts, many of which require audience participation.
- The children are encouraged to read story theater excerpts taken from easy-to-read books.
- The children participate in games that may spin off from the story.
- The children are shown how to check out books from the library.
- The librarians, teachers, and children review the books that are presented and read.
- The librarian presents the library cards with pomp, ceremony, and general hoopla.
- The children are given a tour of the children's book section and shown how to find books of interest.

The "First Grade Roundup" is very popular and successful. Children enjoy especially helping Thomas read the signs that he cannot read in *The Tale of Thomas Mead,* by Pat Hutchins. They also love to help Amelia Bedelia read a list of household chores (the Peggy Parrish series). It is especially exciting that 50 percent of the students continue to use their library cards and to come to the library several years after they have completed the program.

For additional information, see appendixes M and N.

Contributed by
Mary Frydrych, Children's Services Coordinator
Maggie McDaniel, Publicity
and Promotions Coordinator
Kent County Library System
Grand Rapids, Michigan

BOOKS AND BIRTHDAYS

"Books and Birthdays" is a voluntary program in which a child gives a book to the school library on his or her birthday. The contributions add to the number of volumes in the library and encourage children's interest in books.

To implement "Books and Birthdays":

- In the library-media center, display a collection of books that have been donated by other children.
- Create a special bookplate, which includes the child-donor's name, to place inside the front cover of each donated book.
- Make the presentation of the bookplate (to be placed inside the book) in the child's classroom on his or her birthday.
- Accompany the presentation with the singing of "Happy Birthday."
- Express appreciation to the child for his or her gift.

The voluntary giving of books enhances the shelves of the library and gladdens the hearts of the children.

Contributed by
Jane Viere, Library-Media Specialist
Cotton Creek Elementary School
Westminster, Colorado

A FAMILY–PUBLIC LIBRARY READ-ALOUD

The children's librarians of the Shoreham-Wading River Public Library, Shoreham, New York, have developed a program they call "Families Who Read Aloud Read a Lot." Inspired by Jim Trelease's *The Read Aloud Handbook,* the librarians began their program in April, 1985, during National Library Week.

To promote their plan, the library staff did the following:

- Engaged a local artist to create an eye-catching logo
- Sought the help of the Friends of the Library to sell T-shirts celebrating the program
- Prepared Read-Aloud kits complete with bibliographies, pamphlets, and other materials
- Wrote publicity releases for various media
- Created a library display
- Contacted PTA groups to announce the program at elementary and middle schools
- Distributed letters to teachers in the schools
- Sent letters home to parents
- Provided Read-Aloud T-shirts to be worn by the staff

After the preparation and publicity, two activities to attract families were offered: A storyteller told stories from around the world, and a pizza reading party was given for children and their parents. Already, 125 families have participated, and the program continues to expand. Additionally, other libraries have caught the spirit and have made the program available. To date, over 90 libraries are providing "Families Who Read Aloud Read a Lot." The librarians and the families who participate have found excitement and fun at the library.

The Read-Aloud kits contain the following:

- A bright, cheerful pen
- A red and white bumper sticker, "Have You Read to Your Child Today?"
- A bookmark with a poem about sharing the love of reading
- A Read-Aloud memory book for recording and commenting on books

- A newsletter that includes book reviews by participating families
- Blank forms for book reviews
- Handouts from the American Library Association
- Three short lists of books for six age groups: Contemporary Classics, Read-Aloud Favorites, and Families Who Read Aloud Read a Lot
- Articles on reading aloud by Loretta Piscatella, E. L. Konigsberg, Erma Bombeck, and Fred M. Hechinger.

Contributed by
Lori Blend, Marie Orlando, and
Margery Scheidet, Children's Librarians
Shoreham-Wading River Public Library
Shoreham, New York

BOOK BUDDIES AND MORE

The Children's Services section of the San Francisco Public Library provides quality programs for children, with special emphasis on activities that are appropriate for language minority children. Some of the most successful of these are listed below:

- Book Buddies—The library staff trains volunteers to read to children in pediatric hospitals and clinics. Fifty volunteers read to over 300 children each week. The program has received honors and attention from the media and associations for children's health care.
- Dial a Story—Children may dial a toll-free number to hear stories in English, Spanish, or Cantonese. The stories are popular with and suitable for children ages three to five years.
- Video Club—Children learn to design commercials for the library. They are also taught to film library activities and to design video productions. Children enjoy presenting short promotions of reading and using the library.
- Spanish Book Talking—The staff of the Mission District Branch of the library has visited bilingual classrooms and talked about reading in Spanish. The Spanish Book Talking plan has captured a new audience of children.
- Cooperative Summer Reading Program—The San Francisco Unified School District and the San Francisco Public Library cooperate in support of summer reading. The library prepares book lists for distribution among the schools. The schools, in turn, offer incentives for students to visit the library, read books, and join the summer reading program.

Contributed by
Neel Parikh, Coordinator of Children's Services
San Francisco Public Library
San Francisco

BOOKS ON THE MOVE

Staff members of the San Mateo (California) Public Library visit children who are unable to visit the library. All the classrooms for kindergarten through grade eight receive visitors from the library staff twice a year. During the first visit, the librarians tell stories, read books, present puppet shows, and talk about books. On the second visit, they tell the children about the library's summer reading program. The children are encouraged to set goals for their reading and to reach those goals.

Librarians also take the bookmobile to day care centers once a month. They tell stories and circulate books. A particularly valuable outreach has been their visits to latch-key children's programs at school sites; children are encouraged to come to the library and to receive new library cards.

In nearby Mountain View, librarians believe that books and children belong together, and they work closely with schools and parents to achieve that "magical connection."

Contributed by
Linda Holtslander-Burton, Coordinator of
Children's and Young Adults' Services
San Mateo Public Library
San Mateo, California

Karin Bricker, Senior Librarian,
Children's Services
Mountain View, California

THE BATTLE OF THE BOOKS

The "Battle of the Books" is a competition similar to television's "Quiz Bowl." The students are asked to answer questions about books they have read, and they earn points for their responses. Certificates are given for participation, finalists are selected, and prizes are awarded. The competition is organized to stimulate and to integrate the skills of listening, speaking, reading, and writing.

A similar activity is conducted in the Maumee, Ohio, schools. That competition is structured as follows:

- The elementary-level librarians visit the third, fourth, and fifth grade classes each spring and show videotapes or slides of the previous year's "Battle."
- At the end of the school year, each student receives a book list for summer reading.
- Parents of third, fourth, and fifth grade students receive a letter describing the program and its objectives.
- A teacher from each elementary building is responsible for the details of organizing the current year's "Battle."
- Several teachers create questions from approximately 50 books that are suitable for students in grades four and five.
- Through both oral and written competitions, the students with the greatest knowledge of the books are identified.

- Three finalists are selected from each grade level at each participating school.
- All students who have read ten or more books receive certificates.
- The books that are under discussion are placed on display the evening of the "Battle."
- Librarians and teachers from the participating schools serve as the judges, and the district superintendent acts as the moderator.
- The parents and community members are invited to view the "Battle."
- The winners are announced, and they receive prizes—books donated by the local bookstores.
- Refreshments are served to make the event a festive and joyous occasion.

The "Battle of the Books" has increased the students' interest in books and has created excitement about reading not only during the summer but also throughout the year.

For additional information, see appendixes O and P.

Contributed by
Ida May Sonntag
Department Chairperson
Fort Miami School
Maumee, Ohio

THE ENDLESS CHAIN OF READING

The Media Services staff of Consolidated School District, New Britain, Connecticut, created "The Endless Chain of Reading" during National Library Media Month. Students earn chains for each book they read. The chains are made from strips of construction paper and contain the name of the book, the author, and the reader. The students place their chains in the media centers of their schools and enjoy seeing the chains grow before their very eyes. Teachers, principals, and other school personnel are invited to contribute to the endless chain. Although no prizes are awarded, the chains generate great excitement and interest as new links are added daily. Eventually, the chains from all ten schools are brought together in the office of the central administration building. In a presentation to the district superintendent, the endless chain is looped around and around the walls of the board of education's meeting room. Two students from each school and the media specialist make the presentation. The festivities include newspaper coverage, picture taking, informal talks with the superintendent, and refreshments. One year, a grand total of 17,489 books were read and entered on one chain.

Schools that wish to create their own endless chains may follow this plan:

* Arrange to promote the links for the chain to coincide with a local or national event in reading.
* Tell the teachers and students about the plan.
* Make available the construction paper (6- x 2-inch strips) (15.2 x 2.5 centimetres), pens, and staples to form the links.
* Ask students to write the titles of their books, the authors' names, and their own names on the links.
* Hang the chains in the school media center or in another suitable prominent place at each school.
* Arrange to collect all the chains at the end of the time period.
* Plan a formal presentation to the school board and superintendent.
* Select representatives from the schools to take part in the ceremony.
* Encourage media coverage, picture taking, and other appropriate festivities to mark the occasion.

Contributed by
Edward Murratti, Coordinator of Media Services
New Britain Public Schools
New Britain, Connecticut

INSIDE AND OUTSIDE A BOOK

At Addams Elementary School, Fresno, California, the library staff plans a variety of special activities to keep children wanting to come back to the library often. The staff offers these enticements:

* Special bookmarkers made by staff and students
* Favorite book covers made by students and placed on display in the library
* New books given to students whose names are drawn
* Displays of books about different countries

The library is made attractive, inviting, and warm and cozy, like a good book, so that the students will want to come back again and again.

Contributed by
Lenore Daw, District Librarian, K–12
Sharron Pemberton, Library Technician
Addams Elementary School
Fresno Unified School District
Fresno, California

A READERS' GROUP FOR HIGH SCHOOL

At Point Huron (Michigan) High School, a readers' group meets weekly before school and enjoys the following activities:

- Discussions of books—both likes and dislikes
- Publication of a newsletter, *Book Look,* which contains book reviews and accounts of the group's activities
- Storytelling and other book-related projects at the nearby elementary school
- Introductions to literary terms, books of lasting value, and contemporary books

After reading Victorian novels, the group had lunch at and a tour of a renovated Victorian inn in the community.

Contributed by
Mary Anderson, Media Specialist
Port Huron High School
Port Huron, Michigan

COLOR CODING

In Toledo, Ohio, concern about library patrons whose limited reading skills might prevent their finding suitable materials led to the development of "Color Coding." The staff of the Toledo-Lucas County Public Library received a grant which enabled them to purchase a variety of nonprint media. The materials are color coded, by level of reading difficulty, to help new adult readers find the appropriate levels. The media are arranged in a comfortable, attractive center and made easily accessible to reluctant readers. The library meets the interests and needs of these patrons as follows:

- The media include videos, audiotapes, films, and computer software.
- The basic skills in reading, writing, and mathematics are emphasized.
- The Reading Enrichment Center is arranged so that the collections are in a central, convenient location.
- The center is equipped with audio carrels, VHS carrels, and computers.
- The local Laubauch literacy volunteer tutors are available to assist patrons who request additional help.
- The library's staff members offer advice and assistance in selecting and using the equipment.

The nonthreatening aspect of beginning with this approach to reading has proved popular. Sensitive adults who are basically new readers find encouragement and acquire skills through nonprint formats which, in time, may lead them successfully to print materials.

Contributed by
Susan Coburn, Head
Literature Department

Pat Lora, Department Head
Visual Serivces
Toledo-Lucas County Public Library
Toledo, Ohio

The city goes
So wide and far!
And like a rainbow
Or a star
I cannot see
Around the bend.
I wonder
Does it
Have an end?

Barbara Young

CELEBRATING AROUND THE TOWN

READ-ALOUD CELEBRATION

I HAVE A DREAM

**GIRL SCOUT CALIFORNIA
READING RANGER PATCH**

COMMUNITY INVOLVEMENT

BOOK IT

THE NEIGHBORHOOD IS A "BOOK," TOO. CHILDREN STROLL DOWN STREETS WHERE signs tell them what to do (STOP) and what not to do (DO NOT ENTER). They discover where hamburgers are sold, they see windows full of items labeled to entice them (pizza, toys, pets), and they wonder about the activities in impressive buildings (the post office, city hall, police station). As children wait in the offices of dentists or physicians, they browse through periodicals and magazines, old and new. Community displays, radio and television productions, local newspapers, and commercial enterprises provide a setting in which written language is everywhere. Long before children participate in formal programs of reading and writing at school, they begin to process print and to recognize its power.

Towns that are alive with the spirit stretch from Massachusetts to California. In Springfield, Massachusetts, the community celebrated part of its three-hundred fiftieth anniversary with a "Read-Aloud Celebration." A neighborhood meeting place in East Harlem, staffed by a professional social worker and community volunteers, became a youth action center for the "I Have a Dream" program. The Girl Scout Councils of California encourage reading through their program titled "Earning a Girl Scout California Reading Ranger Patch."

"Community Involvement" in Bradbury, California, promotes interest and involvement in the National Reading Initiative by suggesting an impressive array of local activities. "Book It," a national reading incentive program for students in the elementary grades, rewards children for their reading accomplishments.

Fortunate, indeed, are children who live in such cities and towns, because their reading horizons will have no limits.

READ-ALOUD CELEBRATION

In Springfield, Massachusetts, as part of the town's three-hundred fiftieth anniversary, a "Read-Aloud" program was promoted in the schools and homes of children in kindergarten through grade four. The program involved the active participation of the whole community and generated excitement from the mayor's office to the homes of senior citizens. Volunteers were given work-release time from city government offices and from local businesses to participate. Jim Trelease, author of *The Read-Aloud Handbook,* trained the volunteers. From October through December, 1986, 375 classrooms in 29 schools enjoyed readings given by community volunteers. The spirit of reading aloud sparked a movement that took on a life of its own. The mayor proclaimed Springfield Read-Aloud Day, and reading aloud cast its spell.

A blueprint for a "Read-Aloud Celebration" follows:

- Decide on a period of time in which the activity is to take place.
- Announce the plan to all participants.
- Enlist the support of the key personnel in city government—mayor, city council members, supervisors, and so on.
- Share the plan with local businesspeople and request their cooperation.
- Recruit volunteers as readers from every sector of the community—government, business, retired persons, parents, and so forth.
- Publicize the "Read-Aloud" through billboards, bus signs, and bumper stickers.
- Provide written information in the languages of the community—English, Spanish, Korean, Vietnamese, and so on.
- Solicit program sponsors for funds as needed.
- Train the volunteer readers to carry out the program in classrooms.
- Ask library personnel and teachers to select suitable books for reading.
- Request from the local government a proclamation for a specific "Read-Aloud" day and time.
- Prepare follow-up information for parents and others who wish to continue the program.

Contributed by
Helaine D. Sweet, Supervisor
Judith D. Kelly, Coordinator of Special Events
Springfield School Volunteers
Springfield, Massachusetts

I HAVE A DREAM

The uniquely structured "I Have a Dream" program has made the dream of a college education come true for many students. This program was initially run in East Harlem, New York, but today it is found in more than 15 cities across the country. Eugene Lang, a millionaire industrialist, realized that scholarships providing funds would not be enough for students who have little educational motivation and are poorly prepared academically. He announced his offer of college financing to sixth grade students, telling them to stay in school and find a dream for themselves. He then arranged for a social worker, a tutor, and volunteers to provide support for the students in a youth action center in Harlem. Begun with 61 students, the program continues to expand as more and more community leaders follow Mr. Lang's example.

The "I Have a Dream" program, appropriately based on the words of Martin Luther King, Jr., is characterized by a distinctive combination of attributes:

- The student becomes known personally by the sponsor, who combines with affection and concern the support of personal resources and community position.
- The student enters the "I Have a Dream" relationship at a critical point in life, when graduating from elementary school. The relationship is stable, enduring, and committed for a ten-year period, through secondary education and college.
- The student becomes identified as a dreamer and as a member of a special group that generates a strong support network of peers and parents.
- The student has a person, the sponsor, to turn to and to discuss educational, career, and personal problems.
- The student learns to cultivate self-esteem and to sustain the motivation to stay in school and work toward personal goals.
- The student and sponsor are relatively free to respond as individuals to the demands of each situation.

The "I Have a Dream" program continues to grow as new sponsors, with the help of the I Have

(continued)

a Dream Foundation in New York, establish local projects. This program bears testimony to the simple, but beautiful, truth that one person can make a difference.

Contributed by
Kristina Lang
I Have a Dream Foundation
New York

GIRL SCOUT CALIFORNIA READING RANGER PATCH

Girl Scouts in California discover the joy of reading and earn the Reading Ranger Patch for their discovery. The requirements differ for the Brownie, Junior, and Cadette levels of the Girl Scouts, but all of them follow a plan which leads them to the Reading Ranger Patch and to the enjoyment of good books.

Many of the Reading Ranger recommendations are listed here in brief form. For more detailed descriptions, contact the office of the local Girl Scout Council. Girl Scouts are asked to do some of these activities:

- Locate a library in the neighborhood.
- Prepare a scrapbook for keeping notes, drawings, and other "Ranger" information.
- Visit the school library and the closest public library, and find the children's book section in each.
- Note the days and hours of the libraries.
- Ask about the services provided by the children's librarian.
- Draw a map which shows the location of the library in relation to other important places in the neighborhood—home, school, and the meeting place. Enter relevant information in the scrapbook.
- Examine the lists of books in *Recommended Readings in Literature, Kindergarten Through Grade Eight* (Sacramento: California State Department of Education, 1986). List the titles of books that are of interest and write any comments about them that are appropriate.
- Find one book that is on the "Core and Extended Materials" list of *Recommended Readings,* check it out, and read it.
- Find one book that is on the "Recreational and Motivational Materials" list, check it out, and read it.
- Find one book that is on the "Materials for Students in Grades Seven and Eight" list, check it out, and read it.
- Select and read one book about a project of interest.
- Add to the scrapbook information and comments about all of the books read from the various sections in *Recommended Readings.*

- Read a book to another Girl Scout and discuss the book.
- Read a book to an adult—parent, grandparent, aunt, or uncle—and discuss the book.
- Share a picture book with a younger child, listen to the child's response, and talk about the pictures.
- Record all of the reading experiences in the scrapbook, such as reading to a Scout, an adult, or a younger child.
- Use a picture book as a stimulus to write a story. Read the original story to the Girl Scout troop.
- Write a letter to another Scout to recommend a book.
- Rewrite the ending of a story and change the title.
- Write book reviews and include personal comments about the books.
- Read poetry selections and memorize poems for recitation to the troop.
- Write original poems and share them with members of the troop.

- Read about famous women and share what may be learned from their lives.
- Create a personal list of recommended readings and annotate the list from a personal viewpoint.
- Enter each of the activities as completed with identifying information—title, author, personal response—in the scrapbook.

Girl Scouts develop the potential for leadership in communities. Imagine the background of knowledge and skills which become a vital part of each Girl Scout as she earns a Reading Ranger Patch.

Contributed by
Girl Scout Councils of California

COMMUNITY INVOLVEMENT

In Bradbury, California, there is a belief that communities can make a substantial difference in the education of the nation's youth. Several practical and admirable ideas from that community for promoting a national reading initiative are described below:

- Promote a win-win partnership between the school district and local businesses.
- Encourage stores to display books identified in the California Reading Initiative.
- Solicit donations for the purchase of books for schools, libraries, or classrooms. Give public recognition and appreciation to the stores and businesses that donate.
- Make known to parents the names of stores that sell good books.
- Remind parents and others about the book displays in drugstores, supermarkets, and shops that have been part of the back-to-school promotion.
- Suggest that community members look for the displays of various publishers that have put together an assortment of recommended books.
- Ask librarians and art specialists to join forces in developing a response to literature through art.
- Use recreational centers as places where summer reading classes may be offered.
- Encourage after-school reading in an after-school reading club.
- Urge local banks, utilities, agencies, and the like to develop bookmarks with statements in support of reading good literature.
- Request public service announcements on local television and radio stations to let the community know of relevant events in the area.
- Raise funds through book fairs and PTA activities to purchase books for the school libraries.
- Remind local physicians and dentists to have quality reading material for children in their waiting rooms.
- Describe the intent of the National Reading Initiative to community organizations —Jaycees, Kiwanis, Lions, Rotarians—and ask them to consider the National Reading Initiative as a club project.
- Suggest that the local YMCA and YWCA form reading clubs to provide readings, tutoring, read-alongs, and plays for children.

BOOK IT

- Provide training to senior citizens and encourage them to read to children during after-school story hours.
- Obtain good press coverage on all activities, contributions, and efforts of those who help.
- Give public recognition through ceremonies, certificates, and proclamations.
- Ask the local city council and the local school governing board to pass a resolution supporting the National Reading Initiative.

Communities that are prudent and wise enough to implement these recommendations would most certainly help children to blossom academically, be engaged in books, be well acquainted with their literary heritage, and possess the literacy skills needed to be effective citizens.

Contributed by
Beatrice LaPisto-Kirtley, Mayor Pro Tem
Bradbury, California

"Book It" is a national reading incentive program that is sponsored by Pizza Hut, Inc. Students are rewarded for their reading accomplishments with free pizza. Teachers and parents encourage and guide children toward reaching their reading goals. There is no cost to the schools or the students. Information packets are made available to schools in the early spring of each year. The essential ingredients, like those in a good pizza, require some familiar staples and some spicy flavorings:

- Plan the program for grades one through six.
- Set the time period for five months of the school year.
- Ask the teachers to state the goals of the plan.
- Keep a written record of the children's reading on the wall chart.
- Encourage parents to become involved in the children's progress.
- Have children give oral or written reports on their readings.
- Award the free pizza certificates to individual students as goals are met.
- Remind children of the possibility of a pizza party for the entire class.

"Book It" offers many valuable suggestions to teachers on how to manage time, set goals, encourage children, handle reports, and use volunteers. During the 1986-87 school year, over 12 million children were enrolled in "Book It," and that is a lot of pizza.

Contributed by
Eunice Ellis, National Director
Book It! National Reading Incentive Program

Steven S. Reinemund, President and CEO
Pizza Hut, Inc.
Wichita, Kansas

It's nice to know when I'm in bed
That across the world
It's day instead—
And children there are having fun
While it's their turn
To have the sun.

Kathryn Jackson

CELEBRATING AROUND THE WORLD

DISCOVER STORYTELLING
•
READING CIRCUS
•
AND MORE BEARS
•
PASSPORT TO LITERATURE
•
REDISCOVERING FAIRY TALES
•
ROYALTY—AT HOME
AND ABROAD
•
MONKEY MANIA
•
READASAURUS
JUNIOR GENIUS CLUB
•
OTHER PEOPLE—OTHER PLACES

BOOKS HAVE THE POWER TO TAKE CHILDREN TO EXOTIC, FARAWAY PLACES. FROM pages of print come all manner of people so excitingly different from the people in children's experiences. The mystery of the jungle, the ceremony at court, the rites of passage in the tribal village, wild animals in their natural habitats—all beckon the readers to discover the world beyond their homes and neighborhoods. Fantastic tales of travel to places far from earth into the unknown dimension of space also invite children to fasten their helmets and buckle their seatbelts as they lift off into the realm of the stars. Endless wonders await the boys and girls who are soon to enter the twenty-first century. The stories that were make-believe for their parents will be real for them. Created in a rush of inventions and a tumult of technology, a new world awaits. How better to prepare for the marvels of the future than to enter that wide, wonderful universe in books?

"Discover Storytelling" allows children to build their own mental images of people and events as they listen to stories. The poetic, rich language challenges the senses and serves as a strong *antidote* to the canned words and images of television. The "Reading Circus" is also offered as an attractive choice among many activities that compete for children's time and attention. The "Reading Circus" is filled with delightful festivities that capture and hold the attention of children and their parents.

"And More Bears" features a Browsie Bookbear mascot and several friendly little bears that encourage students to read. The center for the bears is called the *Libeary,* and often the person telling stories is in a bear costume. Children come to tea, they write letters to "bear friends," and they learn how to find their way around reference materials.

The "Passport to Literature" program emphasizes fairy tales from many lands. The students record their travels in their passports and locate on a world map the countries from which the stories come. Another plan for using fairy tales involves the writing of original fairy tales. In "Rediscovering Fairy Tales," children learn to develop a story structure and follow a model as they write their introductions, develop their plots, and write the conclusions to their stories.

"Royalty—At Home and Abroad" has enjoyed great popularity for over 12 years. The children in grades four through eight compete for the honor of being recognized as Royal Readers. Special certificates of recognition, pins, and invitations to a reception for special authors are the rewards the children may receive.

During an annual six-week reading marathon, "Monkey Mania" seeks to establish reading patterns that will be long lasting. The children are encouraged to read, read, read and to record the number of pages they have read on the Monkey Record Sheet. Children are awarded extra points for choosing reading instead of television as a leisure-time activity. When students have read 1,000 or more pages, they are invited to a banana split party. Books and gift certificates are given as prizes, but the golden reward in "Monkey Mania" is the habit of reading.

The "Readasaurus Junior Genius Club" encourages children to become specialists, experts, or geniuses in a particular field. Students select their topics, plan their strategies for developing knowledge and skills, and decide on the level of expertise they wish to attain.

The "Other People—Other Places" program is based on a computer theme and computer language—Input: books, Output: the universe. Children read books from the media center, participate in small-group discussions, and report on books that they have read. Special assemblies star Book-Tron, the Reading Robot, and Dr. Oscar Bibliostein. The students travel far and wide without ever leaving home.

On the following pages are ideas for celebrating both earth and the galaxy. In the words of Robert Louis Stevenson, "The world is so full of a number of things, I'm sure we should all be as happy as kings." The whole world, indeed the universe, summons children to make the journey. Books are the passport to adventures that everyone dreams about. No one should miss this rare opportunity to enjoy "a number of things."

DISCOVER STORYTELLING

Visualization is an important skill in reading but, unfortunately, too few children have the opportunity to learn this valuable skill. Listening to stories, unlike watching television, requires children to be actively involved in creating their own mental pictures. A story may be told using rich, poetic language to delight its listeners.

Teachers are encouraged to learn to be good storytellers and to follow these steps to storytelling:

- Choose the story to tell.
- Learn the structure of the story and divide it into sections.
- Visualize the setting for the story.
- Imagine the action of the story as if it were taking place on a movie or television screen.
- Read the story aloud; use voice and gestures to project images.
- Learn the story by heart.
- Practice telling the story until it is natural and comfortable.

The classic stories, folktales, and fairy tales from around the world come alive as the children are encouraged to "see, hear, feel, touch, taste, and smell a story."

Contributed by
Elizabeth Rosen, Professor
San Jose State University
San Jose, California

READING CIRCUS

The "Reading Circus" is planned to compete with other demands on children's time and attention—sports, dance, computers, television, and videos. The circus, which had its origin in Europe, serves as a splendid background for an evening designed to encourage reading. Parents, teachers, librarians, and students cooperate in making the "Reading Circus" a festive and successful occasion. Balloons, costumes, parades, and drama await the circus goers. The community members and the news media provide publicity and bookmarks. A circus is always full of surprises and fun.

To have a "Reading Circus," teachers should follow these plans:

- Organize interested parents to coordinate the evening.
- Recruit community members to help.
- Explain the kind of evening to be planned.
- Assign responsibilities for various tasks.
- Invite a local author to talk about writing and publishing.
- Ask an illustrator to discuss art in children's books.
- Encourage a high school drama group to perform.
- Bring in a community theater group to demonstrate stage makeup and face painting.
- Have personnel from the local library present information and sign children up for library cards.
- Arrange a paperback book sale.
- Invite a speaker from the local newspaper.
- Hold a costume contest and parade.

The children and their parents may enjoy as many festivities as they choose. Each presentation is planned for 15 minutes. Students may prepare press releases, radio announcements, bookmarks, and video commercials to publicize the *event*. There is action and excitement under the big top, and everyone is welcome to the "Reading Circus."

Contributed by
Liz Christiansen, Library Media Specialist
Sally K. Ride Elementary School
The Woodlands, Texas

AND MORE BEARS

Bears are the central theme of the reading program at the Resource Center of Saint Charles School, Bloomington, Indiana. The center, named the *Libeary,* has a collection of teddy bears in residence. During story hours, parents or volunteers may wear bear costumes as they tell stories to children in kindergarten through grade three. For reluctant readers, there is an adopt-a-bear plan, complete with photographs, biographical information, and adoption certificates. Children are encouraged to write letters to their teddy bears, to choose a special bear as friend for a day, and to discover bears in other countries.

To replicate the program, teachers might do the following:

- Create a bear corner in the school library, and choose a bear as the mascot for the corner.
- Encourage parents and volunteers to come to the center for story time.
- Visit classes to explain the adopt-a-bear plan. Show photographs, pictures, and certificates of adoption from the program.
- Arrange for children to visit the bears or for the bears *to visit* the children on their birthdays and for other special occasions.
- Use the bear-child relationship for reading about bears, writing to the special bears, and discovering about other bears.
- Encourage the children to use reference sources to learn about bears in China, Australia, Canada, and other countries.
- Give tea parties to which the children and bears are invited.

Contributed by
Ruth I. Gleason, Media Coordinator
Saint Charles School
Bloomington, Indiana

PASSPORT TO LITERATURE

In "Passport to Literature," students visit the lands of enchantment, witches, giants, and fairies through their readings of fairy tales from around the world. They also discover all kinds of strange and marvelous happenings. Students are urged to use the passport and to:

- Choose their favorite fairy tales and read them.
- Find out in which country the tale originated and place a sticker on a world map to show where the country is located.
- Find another fairy tale from a different place and repeat the process.

The fairy tales may come alive at a tea party in which children dress as their favorite fairy tale characters. Everyone loves fairy tales.

Contributed by
Kathleen L. Miller
Sally K. Ride Elementary School
The Woodlands, Texas

REDISCOVERING FAIRY TALES

Fairy tales provide a picture of other cultures and other people. Every fairy tale contains wishes, dreams, and problems common to human beings the world over. Fairy tales provide children with the opportunity to identify problems and to see how problems are solved. Students are encouraged to write their own fairy tales. They develop creative imitations and learn about the structure of a story—introduction, plot, and conclusion. Though they write independently, the students share their stories with partners and discuss their creations in small groups. They also learn to tell a story in the form of an acrostic. They may work in teams and enjoy the contributions of one another.

To use fairy tales as stimuli for writing, teachers may follow this plan:

- Make available a rich collection of fairy tales from many countries.
- Provide time for reading and discussing the stories.
- Teach students to *map* the stories and to recognize their structures.
- Promote students' original writings, using a story as a model, and encourage variations in plot, character, and events.
- Teach students the form of an acrostic. Give them time to experiment with acrostics in small groups.
- Share students' work in discussions, displays, and storytelling.

Contributed by
Jean E. Ekstein
Los Angeles, California

Pattie Shelley
Santa Monica, California

ROYALTY—AT HOME AND ABROAD

For over 12 years, children in grades four through eight in Sacramento (California) County have competed for the honor of being designated a Royal Reader. The competition takes place within each school, where standards of excellence are set. The students participate through reading, giving oral reports, presenting exhibits, and writing book summaries. Special authors are invited as guests, and Royal Readers are given recognition for their accomplishments. The program may be designed at the school level to accommodate the particular student population.

Some general guidelines for the county-level program are the following:

- Invite the office of the county superintendent of schools to serve as sponsor.
- Call on the staff of the county media center to help with the plan.
- Designate key personnel at the school site to set standards, rules, and dates.
- Provide the necessary information to students and their parents.
- Plan to award certificates, pins, and autographed books as prizes.
- Arrange a time and place for and make known the details of the Royal Reader ceremony.
- Arrange a royal reception to include a Royal Guest Author.
- Promote the event through newsletters and public media.

Contributed by
Penny G. Kastanis, Program Manager
Library Media Services
Office of the Sacramento County
Superintendent of Schools
Sacramento, California

MONKEY MANIA

The purpose of a six-week reading marathon in Fair Oaks, California, is twofold: (1) to encourage reading as a leisure-time activity; and (2) to expose students to great literature. The theme of the program varies from year to year. In 1987, for example, the theme was "Monkey Mania." Letters of explanation and lists of suggested books, by grade level, were sent to parents. Prizes were awarded on the basis of the number of pages read and the number of hours spent reading instead of watching television. "Monkey Mania" was a spectacular success: Library circulation increased, parents responded very positively, and students read well over 250,000 pages.

To conduct your own "Monkey Mania":

- Meet as a committee at the school site to set standards, assign responsibilities, and work out the details of the plan.
- Prepare a list of recommended readings.
- Plan a practical method of recording the number of pages the children have read.
- Send an explanation of the program to parents.
- Talk to students and answer their questions.
- Decide on awards, certificates, prizes, and parties.
- Agree on interim prizes when certain milestones have been reached.

For additional information, see appendixes Q through U.

Contributed by
The teaching staff of Dewey Fundamental School
San Juan Unified School District
Carmichael, California

READASAURUS JUNIOR GENIUS CLUB

Students may attain the rank of specialist, expert, or genius in the "Readasaurus Junior Genius Club." The students choose the ranks to which they aspire and follow the plan outlined below:

- Make a written plan or outline to guide the study. Include the activities to be done to become a specialist, expert, or genius. As part of the plan, make a list of questions which are to be answered in the project. The *specialist* must answer four questions, the *expert* must answer six questions, and the *genius* must answer eight questions.
- Read about the topic. List on the bottom of the page the titles of the works read. The minimum numbers of sources to be used for each classification are as follows:

Books:	Specialist, 4
	Expert, 6
	Genius, 8
Magazine articles:	Specialist, 2
	Expert, 3
	Genius, 4
Encyclopedia entry:	Specialist, 1
	Expert, 2
	Genius, 3

- Make a display, collection, diorama, or model with pictures, drawings, photographs, diagram models, specimens, or samples of the topic.
- Meet with other learned scholars and wise persons. Visit with community members who are experts on the topic. List their names below.

_____
_____
_____
_____

- Visit a place in which one can learn more about the topic—zoo, museum, planetarium, aviary, or greenhouse, for example. Write the names of the places visited.

_____
_____
_____
_____

(continued)

- Participate in a Junior Genius Fair at school. Display things about the topic and share your knowledge with other geniuses.
- Give a presentation to the class on your Junior Genius topic. Arrange and schedule this presentation with the teacher.
- View a film, videotape, filmstrip, or the like about the topic. The specialist and expert may use only one source; the genius must use two. List your source(s).

_____

_____

- Join a club, society, or discussion group that has some purpose related to the topic. List the organization(s).

_____

_____

- Write a short book or pamphlet about the topic. Include pictures or even your own illustrations.
- Make up a game or puzzle about the topic. The product should be something to play with other students.
- After working on the project for one month, review the list of questions. Pick out the best one, or write a new one, and then submit it to an appropriate column in the local newspaper.
- Write a poem, play, or essay about the topic or experiences that you encounter while studying the topic.
- Think of an idea that would help anyone learn more about the topic. Write your ideas here.

_____

_____

For additional information, see appendixes V and W.

Contributed by
James Petersen, Principal
Ephraim Elementary School
Ephraim, Utah

Nancy Livingston, State Specialist,
Reading Education
Utah State Office of Education
Salt Lake City, Utah

OTHER PEOPLE—OTHER PLACES

Other People—Other Places" is a reading incentive program designed to encourage independent reading among students in the Santa Ana (California) Unified School District. The program has a computer theme: Input: books—Output: the universe. Children receive awards and prizes for reading and reporting on books from the media center. The program is designed to be practical for teachers to use and enticing for students to participate in.

To implement such a program, teachers may follow these easy steps:

- Give the responsibility for the reading incentive program to the reading specialist, librarian, or other individual.
- Prepare and decorate reading charts and post them in the media center. Enter the names of the children on the charts as they complete their readings.
- Keep a class list of students who have submitted reports on their books.
- Arrange individual and small-group discussions with students about the books they have read.
- Provide at least three levels of report forms to allow for differences among early, beginning, and advanced readers.
- Award prizes at assemblies.
- Plan to have such characters as the Book-Tron, the Reading Robot, and Dr. Oscar Bibliostein hand out the awards.
- Vary the prizes to include certificates, banners, T-shirts, engraved pencils, buttons, books, and magazine subscriptions.
- Give parties and shows for, and hugs to, readers.
- Challenge readers further with contests.
- Make good use of books from other places about other people.
- Create student passports and record students' reading *travels* on them.

Contributed by
Kitty Karp, Reading Specialist
Monte Vista Elementary School
Santa Ana Unified School District
Santa Ana, California

James Autry, English Department Head
Modesto City Schools
Modesto, California

"AUTHOR/ILLUSTRATOR DAY"
COORDINATOR'S RESPONSIBILITIES

The site coordinator (for example, reading specialist, principal, or teacher) will work with the district librarian and the school's media technician. The coordinator may want to form a committee to help with the tasks listed below. It might also be appropriate to involve the school's parent organization as well as staff members.

- Honorarium—The author/illustrator should be paid the honorarium on or very soon after the day of service.
- Meals—The school is responsible for the author/illustrator's breakfast, lunch, and dinner.
  - Breakfast might be at a restaurant, or it could be a staff potluck (juice, fruit, rolls, nutbread, and coffee, for example). Breakfast might also be served in the home in which the author is staying.
  - Lunch might be a staff potluck; cafeteria lunch; catered lunch; lunch for selected students, teachers, and the author/illustrator; lunch at a nearby restaurant; or lunch provided by the PTA.
  - Dinner could be a small dinner party at a local restaurant; a small party in someone's home; room service if the guest is staying in a motel or hotel; or dinner at the host's home if the guest is staying with someone from the school.
- Invitations/bookmarks
  - Design and send bookmarks to the district's printing facility or an outside printing business. Students could handle the distribution.
  - Design and print invitations to be sent to other schools and the guest.
- Publicity/communication
  - Send a letter to parents inviting them to the author/illustrator's presentation.

- Notify the district office and local media about "Author/Illustrator Day."
- Book circulation—Circulate the author/illustrator's books to the teaching staff. The books could be borrowed from other schools, purchased, or checked out from the county library.
- Book ordering—Orders should be placed with the district librarian at least two months in advance.
- Book sales
  - Determine which organization will collect the money and pay the bills (PTA or student body, for example).
  - Determine who will be in charge of book sales. This responsibility is an excellent opportunity for parents' or the PTA's assistance. Be sure to limit the number of people directly involved with bookkeeping.
  - Determine the prices of the books. Obtain a discount from a publisher or book jobber. Add a charge for tax and shipping both ways, and round the amount off to the nearest quarter to allow for easy change making.
  - Set up a bookkeeping procedure. Count and verify the number of books assigned to the school. Make a separate sheet for each title, with as many spaces as there are copies. As each book is sold, the student's name and class code should be entered on the sheet with the appropriate title. This procedure ensures a way of double-checking if a dispute arises about whether a book has been purchased.

"BALLOON DAY"
STAFF INFORMATION

- Advertise "Balloon Day" by:
  - Presenting dates and rules in the classrooms
  - Passing out a letter to parents which includes dates and rules
  - Sending additional reminders to parents in class newsletters
  - Sending the weekly bulletin home with students to remind parents of this event
- Contact a parent volunteer to help with recordkeeping (once or twice weekly). Students will bring in completed reading slips daily. You may want to display the results on a classroom chart or bulletin board.
- All slips should be turned in by the date decided on earlier.

- Students should fill out "Balloon Day" tags (child's name, school address, and so on) and make class flags.
- One student letter should be distributed. A flyer about having a hot-air balloon as part of the program may be sent home later.
- Check the schedule and map for the time and place of "Balloon Day." Remember to designate a student to carry the class's flag.
- The day before "Balloon Day," have classes practice walking to the designated area and the spots where they will stand.

"BALLOON DAY"
RULES

READING BEGINS _____

READING ENDS _____

BALLOON DAY _____

- Each student must read at least three books on his or her reading level to earn one balloon.
- Students must check with the teacher to be sure the books they read are on their reading levels.
- For each book, students in grades three through six will fill out a slip giving the title, author, illustrator (if given), main characters, and a summary of the book.

- First and second graders will complete as much of the slips as possible and then relate other facts to parents or teachers. How much to expect of students will be left to the teachers' discretions.
- After listening to the story read to them by others, kindergartners will tell the teacher or parents the necessary information that is to be included on the slips.
- The slips will be signed by the teacher or the parents.
- A student who attempts and finishes a book above her or his reading level may receive extra credit. This decision will be at the teacher's discretion.
- There will be no limit as to the number of balloons that a student may earn.

"BALLOON DAY"
COMMITTEE

The "Balloon Day" Committee is responsible for the following:

- Contact any community organizations that may be willing to sponsor this program with a monetary donation or match funds with your school's PTA.
- Contact the media (television, newspaper, or news wire) to cover the events of the day. First, call one month in advance, and then call again one week in advance.
- Order the balloons and helium at least two weeks ahead of time.
- Contact a junior high or high school band to play "Up, Up, and Away" at the ceremony.
- Coordinate parent volunteers for recordkeeping. Make additional copies of book slips available to classrooms.
- Borrow a bullhorn.

- Run copies of and distribute the student letters, flyers, and tags to the teachers.
- Complete a fact sheet for distribution to the media.
- Prepare a map of the playground, showing each class's position.
- Prepare a schedule of events for "Balloon Day" for the school staff and parent volunteers.
- Tie individual student tags with 36-inch-long (91.4-centimetre-long) string and attach them to hangers.
- Pick up the balloons and helium the day before "Balloon Day." It is suggested that a custodian be available to help with the storage of the helium. Check the nozzle(s) and tank(s) to be sure they are in working order.
- Return the helium tank(s) and nozzle(s) to the owner.

"BALLOON DAY"
LETTER TO PARENTS

Dear Parents:

We are going to have a "Balloon Day" Reading Incentive Program at our school this year. Our goal is to encourage students to become more involved in reading for pleasure. Students will have from _____ through _____ to read books in order to earn balloons.

On _____, "Balloon Day," students will release their balloons with notes attached stating how they earned the balloons as well as asking for a reply.

Our rules for this program are as follows:

- Each student must read at least three books on his or her reading level to earn one balloon.
- Students must check with the teacher to be sure the books they read are on their reading levels.
- For each book, students in grades three through six will fill out a slip giving the title, author, illustrator (if given), main characters, and a summary of the story.
- First and second graders will complete as much of the slips as possible and then relate the other facts to parents or the teacher. How much to expect of students will be left to the parents' or teacher's discretion.
- After listening to the story read to them by others, kindergartners will tell the teacher or parents the necessary information that is to be included on the slips.
- The slips will be signed by the teacher or the parents.
- A student who attempts and finishes a book above her or his reading level may receive extra credit. This decision will be at the teacher's discretion.
- There will be no limit as to the number of balloons that a student may earn.

Books selected may be from the school library, the public library, or home. Remember a favorite from your childhood reading days, recommend it to your child, and share the memories of good reading . . . together!

Sincerely,

(Principal)
(Reading Specialist)

"BALLOON DAY"
BOOK REPORT FORMS FOR THREE BOOKS

HAPPY READING!

Name _____

Title of Book _____

Author/Illustrator _____

Main Characters _____

Story Summary _____

_____

_____

_____

_____

_____

Name _____

Title of Book _____

Author/Illustrator _____

Main Characters _____

Story Summary _____

_____

_____

_____

_____

Name _____

Title of Book _____

Author/Illustrator _____

Main Characters _____

Story Summary _____

_____

_____

_____

"BALLOON DAY"
STUDENT'S LETTER TO PARENTS

Dear _____ :

_____, _____, is "Balloon Day" at _____
_____ School. I read _____ books and earned _____
balloons.

   Altogether, everyone at school earned over _____ balloons! We are going to have a big
ceremony and let them all go—up, up, and away.

   Each balloon has someone's name tied to it. We hope the balloons will float far away and
that someone will write and tell us where the balloons came down.

   This year, as a special treat, we will have a real hot-air balloon at our ceremony.

   The newspaper and TV stations have been invited. Won't you come, too? It starts at
_____.

Love,

_____

"RECITE-A-POEM CONTEST"
STAFF INFORMATION

- Present the guidelines of the "Recite-a-Poem Contest" to the students.
- A list of authors and poetry that has been compiled by the reading specialist and media technician may help to build a student's background knowledge in poetry.
- Discuss with students:
  - Appropriate selection—topic and length
  - Staging of the presentation—gestures, props, and costumes or clothing

- Promote the contest by handing out flyers to the students and having a bulletin board in your classroom that advertises the contest.
- Be sure all finalists have their names on their poems when they turn them in by the due date.
- Make decorations for the stage; for example, a large valentine.

"RECITE-A-POEM CONTEST" COMMITTEE

- Select a theme or holiday for the contest (for example, choose Valentine's Day and use a red and pink motif with hearts).
- Promote the contest with incentive bulletin boards, flyers, newsletters, and support from teachers.
- Select five judges, preferably reading specialists, one for each of these five criteria:
  - Stage presentation
  - Memorization
  - Enunciation
  - Personal interpretation
  - Appropriateness of selection

- Select prizes for acknowledging participants:
  - Balloons—one blown-up balloon on a stick for each participant
  - Certificates—one for each participant. Seals with ribbons might be used as prizes for first-, second-, and third-place winners at each grade level.
  - Ribbons—one for each participant
  - Books of poetry for first-place winners at each grade level
- Prepare news releases for newspapers.
- Plan the set-up and decorations—a PA system with an adjustable microphone, tables for judges, and so on.

"RECITE-A-POEM CONTEST"
MEMORANDUM TO TEACHER

Date:

To:

From:

Subject: "Recite-a-Poem Contest"

Today begins the process of your students' selecting, memorizing, and presenting a poem or suitable verse-story. The number of Shel Silverstein poems should be limited to one per class. Students should be encouraged to choose from the classics, especially students in grades four through six. Here are the guidelines:

- The speaker first states the title and author and then recites the poem or verse-story.
- The speaker will be judged on:
  - Stage presentation (one prop only, if desired)
  - Memorization
  - Enunciation
  - Personal interpretation
  - Appropriateness of selection
- Three finalists will be chosen by each class, and they will recite their selections at an assembly to be held on _____ at _____ for grades four through six and _____ for kindergarten through grade three.
- Judges will select one winner per grade level. All the winners will receive a prize.
- The names of the class entries must be turned in in writing no later than _____.

"RECITE-A-POEM CONTEST"
MEMORANDUM TO TEACHERS ABOUT DECORATIONS

Date:

To:

From:

Subject: "Recite-a-Poem Contest" Decorations

Plans are well under way for the "Recite-a-Poem Contest" assembly on _____ _____. We could use some help, however, on decorations to make the occasion really festive. We would really appreciate it if your class could make a decoration, perhaps on butcher paper, to put along the front of the stage. Do let your creativity run wild, but limit the height of the ornament to about 3 feet (91.4 centimetres).

"RECITE-A-POEM CONTEST"
FAVORITE COLLECTIONS OF POETRY

Adams, Adrienne. *Poetry of Earth.* New York: Charles Scribner's Sons, 1972.

Poems about the earth and her creatures. Recommended for young readers.

Aiken, Conrad. *Cats and Bats and Things with Wings.* New York: Atheneum Publishers, 1965.

Creative observations about all kinds of animals. Written in unusual shapes and forms. Beautifully illustrated.

Black Out Loud. Edited by Arnold Adoff. New York: Dell Publishing Co., Inc., 1975.

Poems by black poets that are meaningful and appealing to all children.

A Child's Book of Poems. Illustrated by Gyo Fujikawa. New York: The Putnam Publishing Group, 1969.

A lovely book of well-chosen poems with special appeal to young children. Recommended for use in preschool through grade three.

Ciardi, John. *The Reason for the Pelican.* Philadelphia: J. B. Lippincott Co., 1959.

Twenty-three warm, ridiculous poems that children will love.

Ciardi, John. *You Read to Me, I'll Read to You.* New York: Harper and Row Junior Books Group, 1987.

Humorous poems to be read to children. Every other poem is simple enough that a first grader can read it to you.

The City Spreads Its Wings. Edited by Lee Bennet Hopkins. New York: Franklin Watts, Inc., 1970.

Twenty poems about the people, sounds, sights, feelings, and moods of the city. Selected for young children.

Cole, William. *Beastly Boys and Ghastly Girls.* Philadelphia: B. Collins, 1964.

Poems about things children should never do and about boys and girls who lead lives that are neither good nor dull.

Cole, William. *Oh, Such Foolishness!* New York: Harper and Row Junior Books Group, 1978.

Hilarious rhymes and ridiculous pictures about things that never could happen.

Cullum, Albert. *The Geranium on the Windowsill Just Died, but, Teacher, You Went Right On.* New York: Harlin Quist Books, 1971.

Poems that both teachers and children will enjoy. An exposé of the foibles of teachers.

Frost, Robert. *You Come Too.* New York: Henry Holt & Co., 1959.

A group of Frost's poems especially chosen to be read to and by young people.

Giovanni, Nikki. *Ego Tripping and Other Poems for Young Readers.* Westport, Conn.: Lawrence Hill & Co., Inc., 1974.

Poems about being black and about being human. Recommended for use in grades five and up.

Hughes, Langston. *Don't You Turn Back.* New York: Alfred A. Knopf, Inc., 1969.

Selected Hughes's poems about love, hate, hope, and despair. In today's language. Strong appeal for students in junior high and above.

Illustrated Poems for Children. Illustrated by Krystyna Orska. New York: Macmillan Publishing Co., Inc., 1973.

A beautiful anthology, arranged and illustrated superbly. Exposes the reader to many styles, including those of Balke and Mother Goose.

Lear, Edward. *The Complete Nonsense of Edward Lear.* New York: Dover Publishing, Inc., n.d.

A huge collection of crazy, zany poems that are mostly limericks.

McCord, David. *Every Time I Climb a Tree.* Boston: Little, Brown and Company, 1967.

Poems that the youngest readers will want to hear and say again and again.

Merriam, Eve. *It Doesn't Always Have to Rhyme*. New York: Atheneum Publishing, 1964.

Unique, delightful things with words. Plays with sound and rhythm and metaphor will inspire students to love and write poetry.

Miracles: Poems by Children of the English-Speaking World. Edited by Richard Lewis. New York: Simon and Schuster, Inc., 1984.

Poems written by children between the ages of five and thirteen years from many countries. They reveal the rich imaginations and command of the language that children have, and they serve as inspiration for students.

My Tang's Tungled and Other Ridiculous Situations. Edited by Sara Brewton and others. New York: Thomas Y. Crowell Co., 1973.

A delightful collection of tongue twisters and silly poems.

Ness, Evaline. *Amelia Mixed the Mustard and Other Poems*. New York: Charles Scribner's Sons, 1975.

Twenty outrageous poems about silly girls. Beautifully illustrated.

On City Streets: An Anthology of Poetry. Edited by Nancy Larrick. New York: M. Evans & Co., Inc., 1968.

A fine collection of enjoyable poems about the experiences, inhabitants, and scenes of the city. Well-chosen for youngsters.

The Other Side of a Poem. Edited by Barbara Abercrombie. New York: Harper and Row Publishers, Inc., 1977.

Poems with high appeal that are presented in enticing groupings with personal notes to the children.

Poems to Read to the Very Young. Edited by Josette Frank. New York: Random House, Inc., 1982.

Simple, nicely illustrated poems for young children.

Reflections on a Gift of Watermelon Pickle and Other Modern Verse. Edited by Stephen Dunning and others. New York: Lee Lothrop and Shepard Books, 1966.

A favorite collection of poems chosen carefully for young people. A varied selection of works relevant to children's interests.

Sendak, Maurice. *Chicken Soup with Rice*. New York: Scholastic, Inc., 1986.

A short, rhymed story about the seasons for very young children.

Silverstein, Shel. *Where the Sidewalk Ends: Poems and Drawings*. New York: Harper and Row Junior Books Group, 1974.

Fun poems, for children of all ages, about curiosity, naughtiness, mix-ups, warnings, and much more. Every classroom needs a copy of this book.

Some Haystacks Don't Even Have Any Needles. New York: Lee Lothrop and Shepard Books, 1969.

Poems about the real world. Recommended for older students.

Stopple, Libby. *A Box of Peppermints*. Edited by Dick Dromgoole. Austin, Tex.: American Universal Art Forms Corp., 1975.

A collection of poems that touches on everyday things in a child's life: grandparents, animals, mischief, parents, and the elderly. Written from a child's point of view. Appropriate for children in the early grades.

Time for Poetry (Third edition). Edited by May Hill Arbuthnot. Glenview, Ill.: Scott, Foresman & Co., 1968.

The most complete collection of all kinds of poetry on nearly every topic. Includes an excellent section on using poetry in the classroom.

Zaslow, David. *Some Days It Feels Like It Wants to Rain*. Ashland, Oreg.: Kids Matter, Inc., 1976.

An inexpensive little paperback book containing poems about such things as feelings, ice cream, and blue jeans. Contains some especially lovely metaphors.

Zero Makes Me Hungry. Edited by Edward Leuders and others. New York: Lee Lothrop and Shepard Books, 1976.

Full of poems that are alive and powerful and relevant to young readers. Especially recommended for intermediate age and older students.

"FIRST GRADE ROUNDUP" INVITATION TO TEACHERS

You're Invited to the "First Grade Roundup" Celebration

**A library orientation and story program
especially for first grade students
and their teachers.**

The "First Grade Roundup" celebration for your school is scheduled for

_____ at _____ at the _____.
      (date)   (time)   (place)

We hope this is a convenient day for you to come. While we are unable to change the date of your visit, we should be able to adjust the time of day slightly to meet school needs (e.g., 10:30 a.m. instead of 10 a.m. if all teachers agree).

Please let us know as soon as possible of your intention to attend, because space is limited. Call Kent County Library Children's Services at 774-3253. Call us even if you cannot attend, so that we may be able to make adjustments for next year's program. We need your response!

WHAT KENT COUNTY LIBRARY WILL DO

Upon receiving your request to attend at the above date and time, we will quickly send you the number of copies of the child's information booklet that you need. Later, we will process the library registration cards and bring them with us to the program. We also will provide a grand reading celebration for the children, of course!

WHAT YOU CAN DO

After receiving your class information booklets (which include registration cards), you can make arrangements to send the booklets home with your own cover letter encouraging the prompt return of the cards. Once you have the cards back, mail or bring them to:

Kent County Library System
Children's Services
775 Ball St., N.E.
Grand Rapids, MI 49503

We will need two weeks before your program date to process the cards. Your other responsibility will be to arrange to get your children to the program. Hope to hear from you soon.

Any Questions?   Call 774-3253

Kent County Library System

"FIRST GRADE ROUNDUP"
INFORMATION SHEET FOR TEACHERS

"FIRST GRADE ROUNDUP"

Dear _____:

Enclosed are your class information booklets, which include registration cards for your First Grade Roundup Celebration. Your class's First Grade Roundup Celebration is on
_____ at _____ at the _____ library.
　　　　(date)　　　　　　　(time)　　　　　　　　　　　(place)

Here are some ideas we have discovered over the years that will make your Roundup day even more fun:

1. Keep the name tags on the last sheet of the information booklets for each student to fill out and wear to the Roundup. Send the registration cards home with your students for the parents to fill out. Return the filled out cards by _____ to:

    Kent County Library System
    Children's Services
    755 Ball St., N.E.
    Grand Rapids, MI 49503

    We are open from 8 a.m. to 5 p.m. Do not send the cards to the library where your program will be held. Doing so really complicates the procedure. Please call us at 774-3253 if there is a problem.
2. Please return a registration card for every student. The object of "First Grade Roundup" is for each student to receive a library card *at the program.* Children who do not receive cards the day of the program seem very disappointed.
3. Please return the filled out registration cards by class with the *teacher's name attached.* This allows us to distribute the library cards easily to the teachers at the Roundup.
4. You may want to read the featured books to your classes before Roundup day. Classes that are familiar with the stories seem to enjoy the program even more. Our stories are *The Tale of Thomas Mead,* by Pat Hutchins, and *Amelia Bedelia,* by Peggy Parish. We have many copies of these books in all of our branches.
5. You may also want to explain to your students that they will not be checking out books on Roundup day but that they will learn all about the library so they can return with a family member to select materials.

If you have any questions, please call Children's Services at 774-3253. We want to help you and your students to have the best celebration possible.
    See you at the Roundup!

                                        Mary Frydrych
                                        Coordinator–Children's Services
                                        Kent County Library System

"BATTLE OF THE BOOKS"
SAMPLE LETTER TO PARENTS

Dear third, fourth, and fifth grade parents,

Enclosed you will find a list that will be used next November during the Children's Book Week for a competition called Battle of the Books. The purpose of this activity is to encourage summer reading and to familiarize third, fourth, and fifth graders with a variety of books.

We are giving your child an opportunity to get a head start on reading from this book list. In November, some students will be chosen to participate in sharing their knowledge about these books. (It would be helpful if your child kept notes on characters and events in the books for easy recall.)

If your child reads ten or more books from the list during the summer and fall, he or she will receive a certificate as part of Children's Book Week, November 10–14.

Students' reading lists will be due on Monday, November 3. The certificates will be awarded on November 13 at the "Battle of the Books" contest at Fairfield School.

Please encourage your child to become a better student by improving reading skills and to participate in the "Battle of the Books" contest.

Sincerely,
The Battle of the Books Committee

"BATTLE OF THE BOOKS"
SAMPLE READER'S CERTIFICATE

Reader's Club

_____

is hereby awarded a certificate of achievement

for reading _____ books from the

"Battle of the Books" list.

_____
Principal

_____
Teacher

_____
Date

"MONKEY MANIA"
REWARD COUPONS

_____ gets to

monkey around tonight!

This coupon is good for 1 night off from homework. Redeem by January 30, 1989.

750 pages—GREAT!

This coupon has been issued to

_____

It is good for 1 Popsicle. Redeem this coupon promptly with Mrs. Hendrickson.

300 pages—TERRIFIC!

"MONKEY MANIA"
VERIFICATION FORM FOR STUDENT'S READING

Dewey School No TV Day

This is to certify that

_____

Student's name

did not watch TV on Wednesday, October 8.

Check one:

_____   I did not watch TV.
        Instead, I read _____.   25 points

_____   Our family did not watch TV.
        Instead, we read _____.   50 points

_____   _____

Student's signature   Parent's signature

"MONKEY MANIA"
BOOKMARK

THIS
BOOKMARK
BELONGS
TO

_____

"MONKEY MANIA"
INVITATION TO THE BANANA SPLIT PARTY
FOR READING ACCOMPLISHMENT

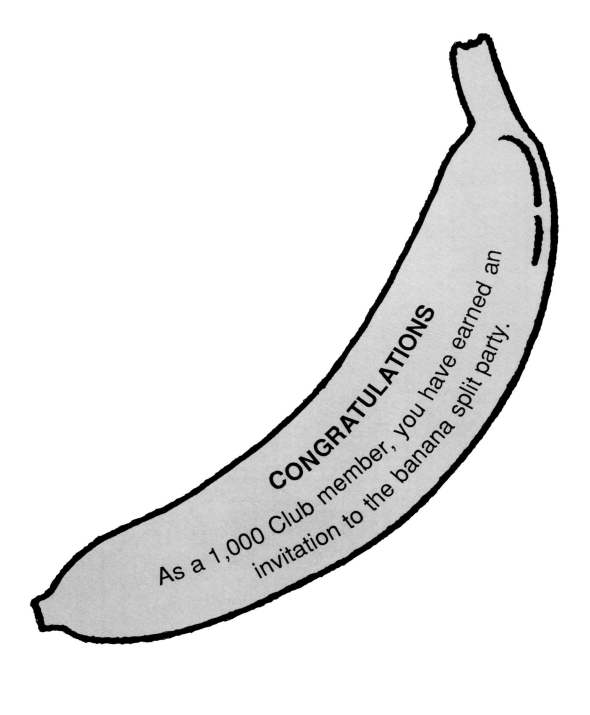

CONGRATULATIONS

As a 1,000 Club member, you have earned an invitation to the banana split party.

(Invitations to the banana split party were done on yellow astrobrite stock and cut by parents.)

"MONKEY MANIA"
RECOGNITION FOR PARTICIPATING STUDENTS

Name

Teacher

"Monkey Mania"
500 Club
Member

(Monkeys were swinging from trees in the library. Ribbons were attached.)

"READASAURUS JUNIOR GENIUS CLUB"
SAMPLE APPLICATION

Readasaurus
Junior Genius Club
Official
Application

I _____ do hereby make application to complete a

Junior Genius Project at _____ School.

In doing so, I agree to adhere to the highest standard of scholarly investigation and to become a true "specialist," "expert," or "genius" in my chosen field.

The topic I have chosen with the help of my parents and teacher is _____

_____.

As a parent of _____ , I am aware of my child's Junior Genius Project and hereby agree to provide support, direction, and technical assistance to my child in this worthwhile endeavor.

_____
Parent's signature

"READASAURUS JUNIOR GENIUS CLUB"
SUMMARY AND SIGN-OFF SHEET

When you have completed work on your Junior Genius Project, fill out this form.

Review your activities with your parents and your teacher, and have them sign below.

Name _____ Date _____

Level achieved _____ Topic _____

Activities completed:

1. _____   6. _____   11. _____
2. _____   7. _____   12. _____
3. _____   8. _____   13. _____
4. _____   9. _____   14. _____
5. _____   10. _____

_____
Student's signature

_____
Parent's signature

_____
Teacher's signature

_____
Principal's signature

RECOMMENDED READINGS

The ideas and activities compiled in this volume suggest many ways that children can be introduced to literature. The books listed below can assist parents, librarians, and teachers in implementing the projects themselves. Readers should be able to find these resources in school or public libraries. In some cases, interlibrary loans may be necessary to obtain them.

Baker, Augusta, and Ellin Greene. *Storytelling: Art and Technique* (Second edition). New York: R. R. Bowker, 1987.

> A how-to guide to storytelling for beginners and professionals.

Bauer, Caroline Feller. *Handbook for Storytellers*. Chicago: American Library Association, 1977.

> One of the best sources of program ideas and techniques, covering all types of activities from puppetry and poetry to storytelling and creative dramatics. Other books by the author include *This Way to Books* (Bronx, N.Y.: H. W. Wilson, 1983) and *Celebrations: Read-Aloud Holiday and Theme Book Programs* (Wilson, 1985).

Bodart, Joni. *Booktalk! Booktalking and School Visiting for Young Adult Audiences*. Bronx, N.Y.: H. W. Wilson, 1980.

> Booktalking—the oral introduction of books to an audience—tips and techniques, plus numerous recommendations and examples. *Booktalk 2: Booktalking for All Ages and Audiences* (H. W. Wilson, 1985) is the sequel.

Carlson, Ann D. *Early Childhood Literature–Sharing Programs in Libraries*. Hamden, Conn.: Library Professional Publications, 1985.

> Examples and suggestions for literature-related programs for young children.

Champlin, Connie. *Puppetry and Creative Dramatics in Storytelling*. Austin, Tex.: Nancy Renfro Studios, 1980.

> The use of puppets in creative drama, including activities based on children's books.

DeWit, Dorothy. *Children's Faces Looking Up: Program Building for the Storyteller*. Chicago: American Library Association, 1979.

> Storytelling tips and sources, with examples of thematic programs.

Kaye, Peggy. *Games for Reading: Playful Ways to Help Your Child Read*. New York: Pantheon Books, 1984.

> A practical handbook for parents and teachers who want to encourage reading as an enjoyable, fun activity.

Kimmel, Margaret Mary, and Elizabeth Segal. *For Reading Out Loud! A Guide to Sharing Books with Children*. New York: Delacorte Press, 1983.

> A guide for parents, teachers, and librarians on the whys and hows of reading books aloud to children.

Larrick, Nancy. *A Parent's Guide to Children's Reading* (Fifth revised edition). Philadelphia: Westminster Press, 1983.

> Recommendations for hundreds of children's books, together with essays on ways of developing a child's reading interests, buying books, and creating a home library.

A Multimedia Approach to Children's Literature: A Selective List of Films, Filmstrips, and Recordings Based on Children's Books (Third edition). Edited by Mary Alice Hunt. Chicago: American Library Association, 1983.

> An annotated list of media versions of more than 500 children's books.

Peterson, Carolyn Sue, and Brenny Hall. *Story Programs: A Source Book of Materials*. Metuchen, N.J.: Scarecrow Press, 1980.

> Picture books are the heart of story hours, but other methods of storytelling (flannel boards, puppetry, and creative drama, for example) can be integrated with them for best effect. Patterns are included.

Polette, Nancy. *E Is for Everybody: A Manual for Bringing Fine Picture Books into the Hands and Hearts of Children* (Second edition). Metuchen, N.J.: Scarecrow Press, 1976.

A variety of ways to use picture books with kids of all ages in correlation with different activities (collages and science projects, for example).

Recommended Readings in Literature, Kindergarten Through Grade Eight, Annotated Edition. Sacramento: California State Department of Education, 1988.

Contains the titles and descriptions of 1,010 classical and contemporary works of fiction, nonfiction, poetry, and drama. Also included are works that students whose primary language is other than English will enjoy.

Renfro, Nancy. *Puppetry and the Art of Story Creation.* Austin, Tex.: Nancy Renfro Studios, 1979.

An excellent guide to innovative puppet creation and use of puppets in storytelling. Ms. Renfro is also the author of *A Puppet Corner in Every Library* (Nancy Renfro Studios, 1978).

Siks, Geraldine Brian. *Drama with Children* (Second edition). New York: Harper and Row, Publishers, Inc., 1983.

How to use creative dramatics to enhance learning.

Trelease, Jim. *The Read-Aloud Handbook* (Revised edition). New York: Penguin Books, 1985.

Stresses the value of reading aloud to children. Includes an annotated list of over 300 recommended titles.

Willson, Robina Beckles. *Creative Drama and Musical Activities for Children.* Boston: Plays, Inc., 1979.

Musical games and songs that may be interpreted through activities.

Ziskind, Sylvia. *Telling Stories to Children.* Bronx, N.Y.: H. W. Wilson, 1976.

A basic introduction to storytelling that also stresses poetry and creative dramatics.

LIST OF CONTRIBUTORS

Alice Addison
P.O. Box 342
Arroyo Grande, CA 93420

Christine M. Allen, Librarian
Chemawa Middle School
8830 Magnolia Ave.
Riverside, CA 92504

Mary Anderson, Media Specialist
Port Huron High School
2215 Court St.
Port Huron, MI 48060

Bonnie Arneson
Marketing
Greenhaven Press, Inc.
577 Shoreview Park Rd.
St. Paul, MN 55126

Harriet M. Atkinson, Coordinator of
the San Benito County Literacy
Program
5450 San Felipe Rd.
Hollister, CA 95023

Rodney Atkinson, Curriculum
Consultant, Music
Office of the Kings County
Superintendent of Schools
Government Center
Hanford, CA 93230

Nancie Atwell
Dogfish Head
Southport, ME 04576

James Autry, English Department
Head
Modesto City Schools
426 Locust St.
Modesto, CA 95351

Dorothy Baird
Los Alamitos Unified School
District
10652 Reagan St.
Los Alamitos, CA 90720-2192

Jane Bandy-Smith, Library Media
Specialist
Alabama Department of Education
Student Instructional Services
Elementary Education Services
111 Coliseum Blvd.
Montgomery, AL 36193

Laurel Barnard, School and College
Marketing Manager
Bantam Books, Inc.
666 Fifth Ave.
New York, NY 10103

Eva Barron, Assistant Language
Arts Supervisor
Teaneck Reading Incentive Program
Teaneck Public Schools
One Merrison St.
Teaneck, NJ 07305

Jane Berkowitz, President
JB Enterprises—New Directions in
Education
65 Glenbrook Rd.
Stamford, CT 06902

Manya Berman
2212 Soledad Rancho Rd.
San Diego, CA 92109

Lori Blend, Children's Librarian
Shoreham-Wading River Public
Library
Route 25A
Shoreham, NY 11786-9697

Pamela Bovyer-Cook
Grass Valley Elementary School
5836 Lawton Ave.
Oakland, CA 94618

Karin Bricker, Senior Librarian
Children's Services
City of Mountain View
585 Franklin St.
Mountain View, CA 94041

Susan A. Burgess, Consultant
498 Oak St.
Westwood, MA 02090

Annie Calkins, Language Arts
Specialist
Division of Educational Program
Support
Alaska Department of Education
P.O. Box F
Juneau, AK 99811-0500

Rebekah Caplan, Codirector
University of California, Berkeley/
Bay Area Writing Project
University of California, Berkeley
School of Education
Berkeley, CA 94720

R. Jean Carlin, Reading Coordinator
D. C. Heath and Company
Elementary Division
Western Regional Office
1450 Grant Ave.
Novato, CA 94947-3195

Marilyn Carpenter
1016 Fifth Ave.
Arcadia, CA 91006

Wendy J. Carr,
Bookfair Chairperson
Oakwood Elementary School PTA
Lodi Unified School District
8844 Ravenwood
Stockton, CA 95209

Liz Christiansen, Library Media
Specialist
Sally K. Ride Elementary School
4920 W. Panther Creek Dr.
The Woodlands, TX 77381

Susan Coburn, Head
Literature Department
Toledo-Lucas County Public Library
325 Michigan St.
Toledo, OH 43624-1614

Bernard Cohen, Managing Editor
Santillana Publishing Company, Inc.
257 Union St.
Northvale, NJ 07647

Amy L. Cohn, Marketing Manager
The Horn Book, Inc.
Park Square Building
31 St. James Ave.
Boston, MA 02116

John Y. Cole, Director
The Library of Congress
Washington, DC 20540

Ann M. Corbett, Reading Consultant
Eliot School
Clinton, CT 06413

Julia Candace Corliss, Reading
 Specialist
The Mirman School
16180 Mulholland Dr.
Los Angeles, CA 90049

John E. Cowen, Director
Office of Curriculum and Instruction
Teaneck Public Schools
One Merrison St.
Teaneck, NJ 07666-0756

Coyle Avenue Elementary School,
 Teaching Staff of
San Juan Unified School District
6330 Coyle Ave.
Carmichael, CA 95608

Susan S. Crum, Principal
McKinley Elementary School
1425 Manley Dr.
San Gabriel, CA 91776

Leona Curhan, National Sales
 Manager
Sundance Publishers and Distribu-
tors, Inc.
P.O. Box 1326, Newtown Rd.
Littleton, MA 01460

Perry Hume Davis II
1067 Palos Verdes Blvd.
Redondo Beach, CA 90277

Lenore Daw, District Librarian,
 K–12
Fresno Unified School District
3132 E. Fairmont Ave.
Fresno, CA 93726

Dewey Fundamental School,
 Teaching Staff of
7025 Falcon Rd.
Fair Oaks, CA 95628

Lois Dotson, Director
Rincon Center for Learning
594 N. Westwind Dr.
El Cajon, CA 92020

Maxine Driscoll,
 Program Administrator
San Francisco Unified School
 District
2550 25th Ave.
San Francisco, CA 94116

Jean Dunham, Principal
Pine Grove Elementary School
Orcutt Union Elementary School
 District
1050 Rice Ranch Rd.
Orcutt, CA 93455

Jeanne Dwyer, Library Technician
Manchester GATE School
Fresno Unified School District
Education Center
Tulare and M Sts.
Fresno, CA 93721

Endama (Vicki) Easley
15150 Magnolia, #229
Westminster, CA 92683

Hilda Edwards, Reading Recovery
 Coordinator
State of Ohio Department of
 Education
Columbus, OH 43266-0308

Jean E. Ekstein
3900 Mandeville Canyon Rd.
Los Angeles, CA 90049

Eunice Ellis, National Director
Book It! National Reading Incentive
 Program
P.O. Box 2999
Witchita, KS 67201

Judith Ellis
Pasadena Unified School District
Cleveland Elementary School
524 Palisade St.
Pasadena, CA 91103

Louise Feinberg, Mentor Teacher
1095 W. Roberts
Fresno, CA 93711

Audrey Fielding, Project Director
Benjamin Franklin Middle School
1430 Scott St.
San Francisco, CA 94115

Bev Forker, Library Technician
Robinson Elementary School
Fresno Unified School District
Education Center
Tulare and M Sts.
Fresno, CA 93721

Esther Franklin
3980 McKinley Blvd.
Sacramento, CA 95819

Evelyn Friedman
Los Angeles Unified School
 District, Region H
P.O. Box 3307, Terminal Annex
Los Angeles, CA 90051

Mary Frydrych, Children's Services
 Coordinator
Kent County Library System
775 Ball Ave., N.E.
Grand Rapids, MI 49503

Barbara Garrop, Project Director
Benicia Unified School District
Mills Elementary School
401 E. K St.
Benicia, CA 94510-3498

Lance M. Gentile, Chairman and
 Professor
Department of Education
University of North Carolina at
 Asheville
One University Heights
Asheville, NC 28804-3299

Ann Glaser, Project Director
FUTUREPRINT
California Demonstration Reading
  Program
De Anza Reading Center
1450 S. Sultana Ave.
Ontario, CA 91761

Ruth I. Gleason, Media Coordinator
Saint Charles School
2224 E. Third St.
Bloomington, IN 47401

N. Jerome Goldberg, Assistant
  Superintendent
Curriculum, Instruction, and
  Assessment
Natick Public Schools
13 E. Central St.
Natick, MA 01760

Jeannette Goshgarian, Library
  Technician
Fresno Unified School District
Sunset Elementary School
Education Center
Tulare and M Sts.
Fresno, CA 93721

Ruth Gottstein
Volcano Press
P.O. Box 270
Volcano, CA 95609

Barbara Guzzetti, Assistant
  Professor
Teacher Preparation Center
California State Polytechnic
  University
3801 W. Temple Ave.
Pomona, CA 91768-4011

Nadine Haddock, Reading/Resource
  Teacher
San Miguel Elementary School
P.O. Box 128
Lemon Grove, CA 92045-0128

James L. Halverson
Modoc County Adult Tutorial
  Program
Modoc County Library
212 W. Third St.
Alturas, CA 96101

Mr. and Mrs. Richard Hanley
43 Gildare Dr.
East Northport, NY 11731

Barbara Hanno, Reading Product
  Manager
Elementary Division
D. C. Heath and Company
125 Spring St.
Lexington, MA 02173

Sue C. Hare, Superintendent
Lower Kuskokwim School District
P.O. Box 305
Bethel, AK 99559

Terrie Harlick
Brownie Troop 1017
316 Kidder Ave.
Grass Valley, CA 95945

Grant Harrison
209 MCKB
Brigham Young University
Provo, UT 84602

JoAn and Bill Hart
Edupraxis Literacy Through
  Literature
5116 Remington Rd.
San Diego, CA 92115

Allan Hartley, Vice President, Sales
  and Marketing
H. P. Kopplemann, Inc.
Paperback Book Service
140 Van Block Ave.
P.O. Box 145
Hartford, CT 06141-0145

Betty Hartley, Reading Teacher
Mt. Ararat Reading Center
Mt. Ararat School
Topsham, ME 04086

Esther Hautzig
505 W. End Ave.
New York, NY 10024

Janice Heirshberg
Jan's Books: Tots to Teens
467 S. Arnaz Dr., #406
Los Angeles, CA 90048

Mary Jo Heller, District Librarian
Brisbane Elementary School District
One Solano St.
Brisbane, CA 94005

Beverley Hendrickson, Principal
Dewey Fundamental School
San Juan Unified School District
7025 Falcon Rd.
Fair Oaks, CA 95628

Alberta Henley, Principal
5421 Marjan Ave.
Los Angeles, CA 90056

Rosemary Herndon
Julien Elementary School
1924 E. Canal Dr.
Turlock, CA 95380

Mimi Hjersman, Director of
  Program Delivery
Tierra del Oro Girl Scout Council
3005 Gold Canal Dr.
Rancho Cordova, CA 95670

Sharon Hoffman, Vice President,
  Marketing
Players Press
P.O. Box 1132
Studio City, CA 91604

Linda Holtslander-Burton,
  Coordinator of Children's and
  Young Adults' Services
San Mateo Public Library
55 W. Third Ave.
San Mateo, CA 94402

Terrie Horlick
316 Kidder Ave.
Grass Valley, CA 95945

Judy D. Isted
Book Bonanza
P.O. Box 364
Oconomowoc, WI 53066

Lee Jenkins, Superintendent
Enterprise Elementary School
  District
1155 Mistletoe Ln.
Redding, CA 96002

Carolyn Jessop, Clerical Support
1 AWP Bannockburn H 101
University of California Extension
University of California
Riverside, CA 92521-0112

Johnson Park Elementary School,
 Teaching Staff of
4364 Lever Ave.
Marysville, CA 95901

Margaret A. Just, Educational
 Consultant
1601 Kenneth Rd.
Glendale, CA 91201

Kitty Karp, Reading Specialist
Monte Vista Elementary School
2116 Monte Vista Ave.
Santa Ana, CA 92704

Maralee Karwoski
14343 Windsor Dr.
Yucaipa, CA 92399

Penny G. Kastanis, Program
 Manager
Library Media Services
Office of the Sacramento County
 Superintendent of Schools
9738 Lincoln Village Dr.
Sacramento, CA 95827

Carol Katzman, Director of Educa-
 tional Services
Beverly Hills Unified School
 District
255 S. Lasky Dr.
Beverly Hills, CA 90212

Judith D. Kelly, Coordinator of
 Special Events
Springfield School Volunteers
195 State St.
Springfield, MA 01103

Leo G. Kerr
1222 Sunbird Ave.
La Habra, CA 90631

Sharon Kosch, Program Unit
 Director
San Francisco Bay Girl Scout
 Council
670 McCormick St.
P.O. Box 2389
San Leandro, CA 94577

George J. Kozacik, Reading/Lan-
 guage Arts Consultant
Great River Area Education Agency
 #16
1200 University
Burlington, IA 52601

Judy Laird, District Librarian
San Juan Unified School District
3738 Walnut Ave.
Carmichael, CA 95608

Kristina Lang
140 Byram Lake Rd.
Armonk, NY 10504

Beatrice LaPisto-Kirtley, Mayor Pro
 Tem
2330 Gardi St.
Bradbury, CA 91010

Catherine Lapsansky, Reading
 Supervisor
Pittston Area School District
5 Stout St.
Yatesville-Pittston, PA 18640

Darlene B. Lefevre
Memorial Boulevard Junior High
 School
Memorial Blvd.
Bristol, CT 06010

Nancy Livingston, State Specialist,
 Reading Education
Utah State Office of Education
250 E. 500 South
Salt Lake City, UT 84111

Gail Long, Chair
English Department
Leigh High School
Campbell Union High School
 District
5210 Leigh Ave.
San Jose, CA 95124

Pat Lora, Department Head
Visual Services
Toledo-Lucas County Public Library
325 Michigan St.
Toledo, OH 43624-1614

Teresa McAndrew, Reading
 Specialist
Pittston Area School District
5 Stout St.
Yatesville-Pittston, PA 18640

Maggie McDaniel, Publicity and
 Promotions Coordinator
Kent County Library System
775 Ball Ave., N.E.
Grand Rapids, MI 49503

Anna McElroy, Coordinator
Children's and Young Adults'
 Services Division
County of San Diego—County
 Library
5555 Overland Ave., #15
San Diego, CA 92123-1296

Jan McKee, Teacher
1232 Tiger Tail Dr.
Riverside, CA 92506

Janet McWilliams, Reading/Lan-
 guage Arts Resource Teacher
San Juan Unified School District
P.O. Box 477
Carmichael, CA 95609-0477

Deborah Mantia
The Great Books Foundation
40 E. Huron St.
Chicago, IL 60611

Judy Martin, Library Technician
Lowell Elementary School
Fresno Unified School District
Education Center
Tulare and M Sts.
Fresno, CA 93721

Sally Martinez, Reading Specialist
Berlyn Elementary School
Ontario-Montclair Elementary
 School District
1320 N. Berlyn Ave.
Ontario, CA 91764

Mary Mastain, Reading Specialist
San Juan Unified School District
7400 Sunrise Blvd.
Carmichael, CA 95610

Mary Lou Meerson, Principal
Avocado Elementary School
3845 Avocado School Rd.
La Mesa, CA 92041-7399

Kathleen L. Miller
Sally K. Ride Elementary School
22 Dunlin Meadows Dr.
The Woodlands, TX 77381

Sue Misheff, Chairperson
Committee on Using Children's
  Literature in the Classroom
Ohio Council—International Read-
  ing Association
1054 Third St., N.E.
Massillon, OH 44646

Warren R. Mitchell, Reading
  Specialist
Alabama Department of Education
Student Instructional Services
Elementary Education Section
111 Coliseum Blvd.
Montgomery, AL 36193

Janice Moore, Principal
Fair Oaks Elementary School
10700 Fair Oaks Blvd.
Fair Oaks, CA 95628

Richard Moore, Librarian
Torrance High School
Torrance Unified School District
2200 Carson St.
Torrance, CA 90501

Susan Morgan
6479 Oakridge Way
Sacramento, CA 95831

Harold Morris, Superintendent
Teaneck Public Schools
One Merrison St.
Teaneck, NJ 07666-0756

Tunie Munson-Benson
3932 Lynn Ave.
Minneapolis, MN 55416

Edward Murratti, Coordinator of
  Media Services
New Britain Public Schools
27 Hillside Pl.
New Britain, CT 06050

James L. Newnum, Elementary
  Reading Consultant
Harper Creek Community Schools
7290 B. Drive North
Battle Creek, MI 49017

Carol L. Nyhoff
2737 Elmwood Ave.
Berkeley, CA 94705

Bonnie B. Oliver, Project Director
American Ticket
KCET-Public Television for South-
  ern and Central California
4401 Sunset Blvd.
Los Angeles, CA 90027

Joanne M. Opdahl, Elementary
  Teacher
43461 Vista Serena Ct.
Lancaster, CA 93534

Marie Orlando, Children's Librarian
Shoreham-Wading River Public
  Library
Route 25A
Shoreham, NY 11786-9697

Anne V. Osborn, Coordinator of
  Children's and Young Adults'
  Services
Riverside City and County Public
  Library
7th and Orange
Riverside, CA 92501

Caryne Dean Palmer
3087 Sierra Blvd.
Sacramento, CA 95864-4930

Susan Paradis, Teacher
Memorial Boulevard School
Memorial Blvd.
Bristol, CT 06010

Neel Parikh, Coordinator of Chil-
  dren's Services
San Francisco Public Library
Office of Children's Services
Civic Center
San Francisco, CA 94102

Clara Park, Director
Title VII Project, Secondary Schools
Torrance Unified School District
3420 W. 229th Pl.
Torrance, CA 90505

Sarah Peckham, Librarian
Parkway Junior High School
La Mesa-Spring Valley School
  District
9009 Park Plaza Dr.
La Mesa, CA 92041-1328

Sharron Pemberton, Library
  Technician
Addams Elementary School
Fresno Unified School District
Tulare and M Sts.
Fresno, CA 93728

Diana Penney, Project Director
Willard Junior High School
2425 Stuart St.
Berkeley, CA 94705

Flory Perini, Language Arts
  Supervisor
The Teaneck Reading Incentive
  Program
Teaneck Public Schools
One Merrison St.
Teaneck, NJ 07305

James Peterson, Principal
Ephraim Elementary School
Ephraim, UT 84627

Judy Piper
6479 Oakridge Way
Sacramento, CA 95831

Steven S. Reinemund, President and
  CEO
Pizza Hut, Inc.
Wichita, KS 07666-0756

Peg Ridley, Project Director
Ontario-Montclair Elementary
  School District
Imperial Junior High School
1450 E. G St.
Ontario, CA 91764

Ann Robyns
6308 Thornhill Dr.
Oakland, CA 94611

Elizabeth Rosen, Professor
San Jose State University
One Washington Sq.
San Jose, CA 95192-0090

Elayne Rosenberg, ECE Coordinator
Palm Springs Unified School
  District
Cielo Vista Community Child Care
  Center
4150 E. Sunny Dunes Rd.
Palm Springs, CA 92264

Carol Rowley, Program Specialist
Instructional Media Services
Cajon Valley Union Elementary
  School District
189 Roanoke Rd., Box 1007
El Cajon, CA 92022-1007

William F. Russell
200 California Hall
University of California
Berkeley, CA 94720

Glen Rutherford, Principal
Chaptnguak Schools
General Delivery
Chefornak, AK 99561

Judy Sasges, Coordinator of Young
  Adult Services
Santa Clara County Library
1095 N. Seventh St.
San Jose, CA 95112

Pat Scales, Media Specialist
The School District of Greenville
  County
Greenville Middle School
16 Hudson Rd.
Greenville, SC 29607

Ross Scarantino, District Principal
  Elementary
Pittston Area School District
5 Stout St.
Yatesville-Pittston, PA 18640

Margery Scheidet, Children's
  Librarian
Shoreham-Wading River Public
  Library
Route 25A
Shoreham, NY 11786-9697

Barbara Schmidt, Professor
Department of Teacher Education
California State University
Sacramento, CA 95827

Penny Schott
Peck Elementary School
San Juan Unified School District
6230 Rutland Dr.
Carmichael, CA 95608

Louise T. Scott, Director
Instructional Improvement
Florence School District
Florence, SC 29501

Lyndon Searfoss, Professor
Arizona State University
Tempe, AZ 85222

Anne B. Seil
1619 Calle Ranchero
Petaluma, CA 94952

Susan Shafer, Editor
Scholastic Paperbacks
Scholastic Inc.
730 Broadway
New York, NY 10003

Dorothy Sheeny, Reading Specialist
Mariposa Elementary School
1605 E. D St.
Ontario, CA 91764

Pattie Shelley
2408 34th St., Unit 5
Santa Monica, CA 90405

Karen Simon, Coordinator
English/Language Arts, Reading
Office of General and Professional
  Education
West Virginia Department of
  Education
Capitol Complex
Charleston, WV 25305

J. Skoff
Whisconier Middle School
17 W. Whisconier Rd.
Brookfield Center, CT 06805

Raymond F. Sleater, Director
Book Service
National Office
Boy Scouts of America, S226
1325 Walnut Hill Ln.
Irving, TX 75038-3096

Linda Smith, Library Technician
Wishon Elementary School
Fresno Unified School District
Education Center
Tulare and M Sts.
Fresno, CA 93721

Solano County Reading Association
1025 Delaware St.
Solano, CA 94533

Ida May Sonntag, Department
  Chairperson
Fort Miami School
716 Askin St.
Maumee, OH 43537

Anne V. Speyer
190 Pomeroy Ave.
Pittsfield, MA 01201

Bonnie Spirit, Author
Avitar Books
P.O. Box 222073
Carmel, CA 93922

Stanislaus Reading Council
Stanislaus, CA 95355

Adrienne Stecher, Teacher
North Sacramento Elementary
  School District
670 Dixieanne Ave.
Sacramento, CA 95815

Barbara D. Stoodt
University of North Carolina at
  Greensboro
1100 Forest Hill Dr.
Greensboro, NC 27410

Dorothy Strickland, Professor of
  Education
Department of Curriculum and
  Teaching
Box 135
Teachers College, Columbia
  University
New York, NY 10027

Helaide D. Sweet, Supervisor
Springfield School Volunteers
195 State St.
Springfield, MA 01103

Pennie Taylor
3980 McKinley Blvd.
Sacramento, CA 95819

Phyllis Taylor
312 Capitola Ave.
Capitola, CA 95010

Robert E. Thomas
Heinemann Educational Books, Inc.
70 Court St.
Portsmouth, NH 03801

Roger Tom, Program Director
San Francisco Unified School
 District
2550 25th Ave.
San Francisco, CA 94116

Jeannette Veatch
930 S. Dobson Rd., #66
Mesa, AZ 85202

Jane Viere, Library-Media Specialist
School District No. 12, Adams
 County
Cotton Creek Elementary School
11100 Vrain St.
Westminster, CO 80030

Grant Von Harrision
Brigham Young University
Salt Lake City, UT 84111

Joanne Wagoner
1764 Kendrick Dr.
La Verne, CA 91750

T. Michael Weddle
Thomas A. Edison Elementary
 School
Grandview Heights City Schools
1241 Fairview Ave.
Columbus, OH 43212

M. Jerry Weiss, Distinguished
 Service
Professor of Communications
Jersey City State College
2039 Kennedy Blvd.
Jersey City, NJ 07305

Nancy Whisler, Education
 Consultant
2020 Seventh Ave.
Sacramento, CA 95818

Judith Wilczak
California Literacy Campaign
Menlo Park Public Library
800 Alma
Menlo Park, CA 94025

Frances M. Williams, Project
 Coordinator
Napa City-County Library
1150 Division St.
Napa, CA 94559

Alice Wittig, District Librarian
Mendocino Unified School District
P.O. Box 226
Mendocino, CA 95460

Jackie Ziff
104 W. Holmes St.
Urbana, IL 61801

John Zlatnik, Teacher
36231 Pecan Ct.
Fremont, CA 94536

Over 650 publications are available from the California State Department of Education. Some of the more recent publications or those most widely used are the following:

ISBN	Title (Date of publication)	Price
0-8011-0275-8	California Dropouts: A Status Report (1986)	$ 2.50
0-8011-0783-0	California Private School Directory, 1988-89 (1988)	14.00
0-8011-0748-2	California School Accounting Manual (1988)	8.00
0-8011-0715-6	California Women: Activities Guide, K—12 (1988)	3.50
0-8011-0488-2	Caught in the Middle: Educational Reform for Young Adolescents in California Public Schools (1987)	5.00
0-8011-0760-1	Celebrating the National Reading Initiative (1989)	6.75
0-8011-0241-3	Computer Applications Planning (1985)	5.00
0-8011-0749-0	Educational Software Preview Guide, 1988-89 (1988)	2.00
0-8011-0489-0	Effective Practices in Achieving Compensatory Education-Funded Schools II (1987)	5.00
0-8011-0041-0	English–Language Arts Framework for California Public Schools (1987)	3.00
0-8011-0731-8	English–Language Arts Model Curriculum Guide, K—8 (1988)	3.00
0-8011-0710-5	Family Life/Sex Education Guidelines (1987)	4.00
0-8011-0289-8	Handbook for Physical Education (1986)	4.50
0-8011-0249-9	Handbook for Planning an Effective Foreign Language Program (1985)	3.50
0-8011-0320-7	Handbook for Planning an Effective Literature Program (1987)	3.00
0-8011-0179-4	Handbook for Planning an Effective Mathematics Program (1982)	2.00
0-8011-0290-1	Handbook for Planning an Effective Writing Program (1986)	2.50
0-8011-0250-2	Handbook on California Education for Language Minority Parents—Chinese/English Edition (1985)	3.25*
0-8011-0737-7	Here They Come: Ready or Not—Report of the School Readiness Task Force (Summary) (1988)	2.00
0-8011-0712-1	History–Social Science Framework for California Public Schools (1988)	6.00
0-8011-0782-2	Images: A Workbook for Enhancing Self-esteem and Promoting Career Preparation, Especially for Black Girls (1989)	6.00
0-8011-0209-x	Martin Luther King, Jr., 1929—1968 (1983)	3.25
0-8011-0358-4	Mathematics Framework for California Public Schools (1985)	3.00
0-8011-0664-8	Mathematics Model Curriculum Guide, K—8 (1987)	2.75
0-8011-0725-3	Model Curriculum for Human Rights and Genocide (1988)	3.25
0-8011-0252-9	Model Curriculum Standards: Grades 9—12 (1985)	5.50
0-8011-0762-8	Moral and Civic Education and Teaching About Religion (1988)	3.25
0-8011-0303-7	A Parent's Handbook on California Education (1986)	3.25
0-8011-0671-0	Practical Ideas for Teaching Writing as a Process (1987)	6.00
0-8011-0213-8	Raising Expectations: Model Graduation Requirements (1983)	2.75
0-8011-0311-8	Recommended Readings in Literature, K—8 (1986)	2.25
0-8011-0745-8	Recommended Readings in Literature, K—8, Annotated Edition (1988)	4.50
0-8011-0189-1	Science Education for the 1980s (1982)	2.50
0-8011-0354-1	Science Framework Addendum (1984)	3.00
0-8011-0665-6	Science Model Curriculum Guide, K—8 (1987)	3.25
0-8011-0738-5	Secondary Textbook Review: English (1988)	9.25
0-8011-0677-x	Secondary Textbook Review: General Mathematics (1987)	6.50
0-8011-0682-6	Suicide Prevention Program for California Public Schools (1987)	8.00
0-8011-0686-9	Year-round Education: Year-round Opportunities—A Study of Year-round Education in California (1987)	5.00
0-8011-0270-7	Young and Old Together: A Resource Directory of Intergenerational Resources (1986)	3.00

Orders should be directed to:

California State Department of Education
P.O. Box 271
Sacramento, CA 95802-0271

Please include the International Standard Book Number (ISBN) for each title ordered.

Remittance or purchase order must accompany order. Purchase orders without checks are accepted only from governmental agencies. Sales tax should be added to all orders from California purchasers.

A complete list of publications available from the Department, including apprenticeship instructional materials, may be obtained by writing to the address listed above or by calling (916) 445-1260.

*The following editions are also available, at the same price: Armenian/English, Cambodian/English, Hmong/English, Japanese/English, Korean/English, Laotian/English, Pilipino/English, Spanish/English, and Vietnamese/English.

86-183 03-0340. 0401. 0417 300 2-89 25M